Practical House Flipping

Essential Guides, Smart Strategies, and Checklists for Effective Property Investment

Anthony Dallas

Disclaimer

This book is provided for informational purposes only and is not intended as a comprehensive guide to house flipping. The author and publisher have made every effort to ensure the accuracy and reliability of the information provided within these pages. However, the information is provided "as is" without warranty of any kind.

The author and publisher do not guarantee any specific outcomes from using the strategies and information contained in this book. Success in real estate investing is subject to a range of factors, many of which are beyond the scope of this book. Readers are responsible for their own decisions and actions, and are strongly encouraged to conduct their own due diligence and consult with professional advisors before undertaking any house flipping activities.

No warranties, promises, and/or representations of any kind, expressed or implied, are given as to the nature, standard, accuracy, or otherwise of the information provided in this book, nor to the suitability or otherwise of the information to your particular circumstances.

The content and illustrations in this book, including any resemblance to logos, brands, or images, are entirely fictional and are not intended to represent any real individuals, entities, products, or events, unless otherwise specified. Any resemblance to actual persons, living or dead, or actual events or products is purely coincidental and unintentional.

The examples, anecdotes, and case studies provided are for illustrative purposes only and do not guarantee similar outcomes. The author and publisher are not responsible for any direct, indirect, incidental, consequential, or punitive damages arising from the use of the book's information.

This disclaimer is not intended to limit the liability of the author and publisher in contravention of any requirements laid down in applicable national law nor to exclude its liability for matters which may not be excluded under that law.

The information contained in this book is accurate as of the date of publication but may become outdated or subject to change. No endorsements of specific tools, services, or companies are implied, and the author and publisher do not receive any compensation for such mentions, unless explicitly stated.

All intellectual property rights are reserved, and this book may not be reproduced in any form without the prior written consent of the author and publisher. The advice and strategies contained herein may not be suitable for every situation and in every geographical or cultural context.

Readers are reminded that the real estate market and related regulations can change rapidly, and the author and publisher do not accept any responsibility or liability for the accuracy, content, completeness, legality, or reliability of the information contained in this book.

CONTENTS

Introduction

Welcome to "Practical House Flipping Essential Guides, Smart Strategies, and Checklists for Effective Property Investment" your guide to navigating the exhilarating world of house flipping. This book is crafted for anyone who has ever entertained the idea of transforming properties for profit — from budding entrepreneurs to seasoned real estate investors.

House flipping, the art of buying, renovating, and selling properties, is more than just a venture; it's a craft that combines financial acumen, market understanding, design creativity, and strategic planning. It's a journey that can be immensely rewarding, both personally and financially, but not without its share of challenges and learning curves.

In this handbook, we dive deep into every facet of house flipping. We inform about the groundwork — understanding the real estate market and identifying properties with untapped potential. We also cover the complex world of financial planning, budgeting, and securing funding, ensuring that your foray into house flipping starts on solid ground.

Then, we move into the heart of house flipping: renovation. Here, we unravel the secrets to effective, budget-friendly renovations that add real value to a property. We address the common pitfalls, provide tips for working with contractors, and guide you through making savvy design choices that appeal to a wide range of buyers.

But flipping a house isn't just about the renovation. It's also about understanding the legalities, managing timelines efficiently, and mastering the art of selling. In these pages, you will find comprehensive strategies for marketing your flipped property and negotiating sales to maximize your profits.

Throughout this book, you will encounter advice, practical tips, and actionable strategies. Whether you're flipping your first property or looking to refine your strategies in the business, this book is designed to be your go-to resource.

So, let's embark on this exciting journey together. With each page, you will gain the knowledge, confidence, and skills needed to flip houses and venture into the dynamic world of real estate. Welcome to the adventure of house flipping — where diligence, creativity, and strategic thinking may turn potential into profit.

Building a Reliable Team

In the world of house flipping, success hinges on more than just your individual skills. It involves building a reliable team, where each member's expertise contributes to the successful completion of your projects. A well-rounded team ensures that all aspects of house flipping—from planning and purchasing to renovating and reselling—are handled efficiently and effectively.

Step-by-Step Guide to Building Your Team

Identifying Key Roles:

Real Estate Agent: Specializes in market knowledge and property acquisition.
Contractor: Oversees the actual renovation work.
Architect/Designer: Brings vision and planning expertise.
Financial Advisor: Manages budgets, loans, and overall financial health.
Legal Advisor: Ensures compliance with laws and regulations.

Seeking the Right Talent:

Evaluating Potential Team Members:

- Conduct thorough interviews focusing on experience, problem-solving skills, and compatibility with your flipping philosophy.
- Consider their communication skills and ability to work as part of a team.

Fostering Team Synergy:

Organize regular meetings to ensure everyone is on the same page.
Encourage open communication and collaborative problem-solving.

Setting Clear Expectations:

Define roles, responsibilities, and deadlines clearly.
Establish quality standards and regular checkpoints for project progress.

Building Long-Term Relationships:

Recognize and appreciate each team member's contributions.
Offer fair compensation and consider incentives for exceptional work.

Conclusion

Building a reliable team is a fundamental step in scaling your house flipping business. It's not just about finding skilled individuals; it's about creating a cohesive group that shares your vision and commitment to quality. With the right team, you can take on more ambitious projects, reduce stress, and significantly increase your chances of success.

Additional Resources

- Books: "The Ideal Team Player" by Patrick Lencioni
- Websites: LinkedIn, Indeed for recruitment
- Local real estate and contractors' associations for networking opportunities.

Checklist

- ☐ Identify key roles needed in your team.
- ☐ Research potential team members.
- ☐ Conduct comprehensive interviews.
- ☐ Set clear roles and expectations.
- ☐ Foster communication and teamwork.
- ☐ Build long-term professional relationships.

Know Your Market: Research Local Real Estate Trends and Demographics

Understanding the Landscape

Step 1: Analyze Market Trends

- Begin by examining the local real estate market's historical data. Look at property values, sales patterns, and time-on-market trends over the last few years.
- Utilize online tools and databases like Zillow, Redfin, or local government resources to gather this information.

Step 2: Study Demographic Data

- Understand who lives in the area. Are they families, young professionals, retirees? Census data and local surveys can provide valuable insights.
- Consider factors like average income, employment rates, and population growth trends.

Step 3: Identify Upcoming Developments

- Keep an eye on future infrastructure or commercial projects. These can significantly impact property values.
- Attend town hall meetings or follow local news for updates on planned developments.

Market-Specific Strategies

For Family-Oriented Neighborhoods:

- Focus on properties with multiple bedrooms and a safe, child-friendly environment.
- Schools' quality in the area can be a major selling point.

For Young Professionals:

- Smaller properties or condos in areas with nightlife, cafes, and easy commute options are more appealing.
- High-speed internet and a home office space can be attractive features.

For Retirees:

- Single-story homes with low maintenance and close proximity to healthcare facilities are desirable.

- Quiet neighborhoods with community amenities like parks or walking trails can be a draw.

Keeping Up with Changes

- Regularly update your research to stay ahead of market shifts.
- Network with local real estate agents, builders, and investors to gather insider information.
- Attend real estate seminars or webinars focusing on market analysis and forecasting.

Additional Resources

- Websites: Realtor.com for real-time market data.
- Community: Join local real estate investment groups on platforms like Meetup or Facebook.

Checklist for Market Research

- ☐ Historical data analysis completed
- ☐ Demographic profile of the area understood
- ☐ Impact of upcoming local developments assessed
- ☐ Property type aligned with the target demographic
- ☐ Regular updates to market knowledge scheduled

Step 4: Evaluate Competition

- Assess the number and types of active listings in your target area. How long are properties staying on the market?
- Look at the features and pricing of recently sold properties to gauge what buyers in the area are looking for.

Step 5: Understand Financing Trends

- Be aware of local mortgage rates and lending criteria, as this affects buyers' purchasing power.
- Explore if there are government incentives or grants available for homebuyers in your area.

Step 6: Monitor Rental Market Dynamics

- If you're considering renting the property, analyze the local rental market. What are the average rental rates? What kind of properties are most in demand?
- Understand tenant demographics and their needs. For example, proximity to universities might be crucial for areas with a high student population.

Leveraging Technology for Market Research

- Use real estate analysis software to track market trends and forecast future changes.
- Engage with online real estate forums and social media groups to get insights and advice from other flippers.

Tools for Effective Research

- Interactive maps to visualize demographic and real estate trends.
- Spreadsheets for tracking and comparing property data.
- Mobile apps for real-time alerts on market changes.

Conclusion: The Informed Flipper

Being knowledgeable about your local real estate market is a cornerstone of successful house flipping. It allows you to make informed decisions about purchasing, renovating, and selling properties. By continuously researching and understanding market trends, demographics, and competition, you position yourself to spot opportunities and avoid pitfalls. Remember, in the dynamic world of real estate, staying informed is staying ahead.

This section provides a comprehensive guide to understanding and leveraging local real estate market trends and demographics in house flipping. It emphasizes the importance of continuous learning and adaptation, offering practical steps, tools, and resources to stay informed and successful in the ever-changing real estate market.

Secure Financing: Understand Your Budget and Financing Options

Laying the Financial Foundation

Step 1: Assess Your Financial Position

- Start by evaluating your current financial situation. This includes your savings, income, expenses, and credit score.
- Determine how much you can afford to invest without jeopardizing your financial stability.

Step 2: Create a Detailed Budget

- Develop a comprehensive budget for your house flipping project. Include purchase price, renovation costs, holding costs, and a contingency fund for unexpected expenses.

- Use budgeting tools or software to track your expenses throughout the project.

Step 3: Explore Financing Options

- **Traditional Bank Loans**: Understand the terms, interest rates, and down payment requirements. Your credit score will play a significant role in this option.
- **Private Lenders**: These can be individuals or groups willing to invest in your project, often with higher interest rates but more flexible terms.
- **Home Equity Line of Credit (HELOC)**: If you already own property, a HELOC could be a viable option, using your existing property as collateral.
- **Hard Money Loans**: Ideal for short-term financing, but with higher interest rates. Useful for properties that may not qualify for traditional loans.
- **Government Grants and Programs**: Some regions offer grants or programs for real estate investments, particularly for properties in certain areas or for specific renovation purposes.

Step 4: Negotiate Terms with Lenders

- Approach negotiations with potential lenders prepared with your financial data and project plan.
- Aim to secure terms that align with your project timeline and budget. Don't be afraid to negotiate for better rates or terms.

Step 5: Consider Alternative Financing Options

- **Crowdfunding**: Utilize platforms like Kickstarter or GoFundMe to raise funds, especially for unique or community-focused projects.
- **Partnerships**: Pool resources with other investors or partners to share costs and profits.

Step 6: Regularly Review and Adjust Your Financial Plan

- As your project progresses, continuously monitor your budget and expenses.
- Be prepared to adjust your financial strategy if unforeseen costs arise or market conditions change.

Financial Planning Tools and Techniques

- Utilize financial modeling software to forecast project profitability under different scenarios.
- Regularly consult with your financial advisor to adjust strategies as needed.

Financing Strategies

For Beginners:

- Consider partnering with an experienced investor. This can provide both financing and valuable expertise.
- Start with smaller projects to reduce financial risk.

- **For Experienced Flippers:**

- Leverage existing assets or previous project profits to finance new ventures.

- Build relationships with private lenders for more flexible financing options.

Managing Risks and Liabilities

- Always have legal and financial experts review your financing agreements.
- Understand the implications of each financing option, including the risks involved.

Additional Resources

- Online Courses: Various platforms offer courses on real estate financing and investment strategies.
- Financial Advisors: Consider consulting with a financial advisor experienced in real estate.

Checklist for Securing Financing

☐ Personal financial assessment completed

☐ Comprehensive budget created and tools for tracking identified

☐ Financing options explored and compared

☐ Legal and financial advice sought for selected financing options

☐ Risk management plan in place

Securing the right financing is a critical step in the house flipping process. By understanding your budget and

exploring various financing options, you can ensure that your project is financially feasible and poised for success. Remember, the goal is to invest wisely, manage risks, and maximize returns.

Preparing for Future Projects

- After completing your project, conduct a financial review to understand what worked well and what could be improved.
- Use the insights gained to better plan for future house flipping projects.

Conclusion: Financing with Confidence

Effective financing is not just about securing funds; it's about making informed decisions that align with your project goals and overall financial health. By thoroughly understanding your financing options, negotiating favorable terms, and being adaptable to changing circumstances, you can confidently finance your house flipping projects. Remember, each project is a learning opportunity, paving the way for future success in the realm of real estate investment.

This section provides a structured approach to understanding and securing financing for house flipping. It emphasizes the importance of thorough financial assessment,

exploring diverse financing options, and maintaining flexibility in financial planning. By following these guidelines, you can ensure a solid financial foundation for your house flipping ventures, ultimately leading to successful and profitable projects.

Find the Right Property: Look for Undervalued Homes with Potential

Identifying Hidden Gems

Step 1: Research the Market

- Focus on neighborhoods with growth potential. Look for signs of development, such as new businesses or infrastructure projects.
- Use real estate platforms to find homes priced below market value, often indicating a potential for profit.

Step 2: Evaluate Property Potential

- Look for properties that require cosmetic updates rather than major structural repairs. These can offer a good balance of cost and value.
- Consider the property's layout and how it can be improved. For example, can an open plan be created? Is there space for an extra bathroom?

Step 3: Conduct Thorough Inspections

- Always conduct a professional home inspection to identify any hidden issues like electrical problems, plumbing issues, or foundation cracks.
- Assess the age and condition of major components like the roof, HVAC system, and windows.

Step 4: Understand Local Regulations and Zoning

- Familiarize yourself with local zoning laws and regulations. These can affect your renovation plans and the property's potential use.
- Check for any historical designations or homeowners association (HOA) rules that could impact your renovation plans.

Step 5: Analyze the Cost-Benefit Ratio

- Calculate the estimated cost of renovations and compare it to the potential increase in property value. Aim for properties where this ratio is favorable.
- Factor in not just renovation costs but also holding costs like property taxes, insurance, and utilities.

Step 6: Plan for Marketability

- Consider the end buyer or tenant. What features are most in demand in the area? This could include outdoor spaces, energy-efficient appliances, or smart home technology.
- Ensure that your renovations align with what's attractive in the current market.

Strategies for Finding Deals

For Beginners:

- Start with less competitive markets to gain experience without high risks.
- Consider attending local real estate auctions or estate sales.

For Experienced Flippers:

- Build a network with real estate agents specializing in distressed properties.
- Explore off-market deals through direct mail campaigns or networking.

Utilizing Technology

- Leverage real estate investment software to analyze potential returns and risks.
- Use mobile apps for on-the-go property analysis and cost estimation.

Additional Resources

- Podcasts: Listen to real estate investment podcasts for tips and success stories.
- Websites: BiggerPockets for a community of real estate investors and wealth of resources.

Checklist for Finding the Right Property

☐ Market research conducted for potential neighborhoods

☐ Properties evaluated for renovation potential and cost

☐ Professional inspections completed

☐ Financing and budget alignment confirmed

☐ Exit strategy (sell or rent) planned based on market analysis

Finding the right property is a crucial step in house flipping. It requires a mix of market knowledge, strategic thinking, and the ability to see beyond the current state of a property. By focusing on undervalued homes with potential and conducting thorough research and inspections, you can increase your chances of a successful and profitable flip.

Remember, the best deals are often hidden in plain sight, waiting for a keen eye to uncover their true value.

Leveraging Expert Opinions

Consult with real estate agents, contractors, and interior designers for insights into what sells in your target area.
Attend local real estate investor meetups to learn from others' experiences and insights.

Motivational Spotlight

Highlight a case where a flipper overcame significant challenges, such as dealing with unexpected zoning restrictions, and still managed to turn a profit through adaptability and resourcefulness.

Tools for Effective Property Hunting

Use GIS (Geographic Information System) tools to analyze neighborhood data and trends.
Implement project management software to keep track of multiple potential properties and their evaluation status.

Conclusion: The Skillful Property Hunter

Finding the right property for flipping is not just about spotting a good deal; it's about seeing the potential that others might overlook and understanding the local market's nuances. It involves careful analysis, informed decision-making, and sometimes a bit of intuition. By mastering these skills, you position yourself to identify properties that offer the best opportunity for a successful flip, balancing risk with reward and aligning with market demands.

This section outlines the importance of selecting the right property for house flipping. It emphasizes a systematic approach, including market research, property evaluation, understanding regulations, and planning for marketability. By following these guidelines, you can enhance your ability to find properties that not only offer potential for value addition but also align with your investment strategy and market trends.

Calculate ROI Potential: Assess the Potential Return on Investment

Step 1: Understand ROI in House Flipping

Definition: ROI (Return on Investment) measures the profitability of your house flipping investment. It's calculated by dividing the net profit by the total investment cost.

Importance: Knowing the ROI helps you assess whether a property is worth investing in and aids in comparing different investment opportunities.

Step 2: Gather Data

Purchase Price: Note the buying price of the property.
Renovation Costs: Estimate all costs associated with renovating the property, including materials and labor.
Holding Costs: Include expenses like property taxes, insurance, and utility bills incurred during the renovation period.
Selling Costs: Account for real estate agent fees, staging, and closing costs.

Step 3: Estimate After-Repair Value (ARV)

Market Research: Analyze recent sales of similar properties in the area to estimate the ARV.
Professional Appraisal: Consider getting a professional appraisal for a more accurate valuation.

Step 4: Calculate Net Profit

Formula: Net Profit = ARV - (Purchase Price + Renovation Costs + Holding Costs + Selling Costs).
Record Keeping: Maintain detailed records of all expenses for accurate profit calculation.

Step 5: Compute ROI

Formula: ROI = (Net Profit / Total Investment Cost) x 100.

Example Calculation: If the net profit is $50,000 and the total investment cost is $200,000, then ROI = ($50,000 / $200,000) x 100 = 25%.

Step 6: Analyze and Compare

Benchmark: Compare the calculated ROI with industry standards or other investment opportunities.
Risk Assessment: Higher ROI often involves higher risk. Balance profitability with risk tolerance.

Step 7: Continuous Learning

Market Trends: Stay informed about the real estate market trends affecting property values and renovation costs.

Additional Resources

ROI Calculators: Use online tools for quick calculations.

Real Estate Seminars: Attend workshops to gain deeper insights into ROI calculation and strategies.

Checklist for ROI Calculation

☐ Gather all cost data.

☐ Estimate ARV accurately.

☐ Calculate net profit.

☐ Compute ROI percentage.

☐ Compare with benchmarks.

☐ Assess risk versus return.

Final Thoughts Calculating the ROI in house flipping is crucial for making informed investment decisions. It requires careful analysis, thorough research, and an understanding of the real estate market. By following these steps, you can effectively assess the potential return on your investment, ensuring profitable and wise house flipping endeavors.

Plan Your Renovations: Create a Detailed Remodeling Plan

Step 1: Define Your Goals

Objective: Determine what you want to achieve with the renovation. This could be increasing the property's value, modernizing the space, or making it more functional.

Target Market: Consider the preferences and needs of potential buyers or renters in the area.

Step 2: Conduct a Property Assessment

Inspection: Hire a professional to inspect the property and identify any structural, electrical, or plumbing issues.

Prioritize: Decide which areas need immediate attention and which can be updated later.

Step 3: Design Your Renovation Plan

Layout Changes: Consider if you need to knock down walls, add rooms, or change the floor plan.

Aesthetic Upgrades: Plan for painting, flooring, lighting, and other cosmetic improvements.

Functional Improvements: Update kitchens and bathrooms, which are key selling points.

Step 4: Set a Budget

Cost Estimates: Get quotes from contractors or price out materials if doing DIY projects.

Contingency Fund: Set aside an additional 10-20% of your budget for unexpected expenses.

Step 5: Create a Timeline

Scheduling: Outline a realistic timeline for each phase of the renovation.

Flexibility: Be prepared for delays and adjust the timeline accordingly.

Step 6: Choose Your Team

Contractors: Select experienced and reliable contractors. Check references and past work.
DIY Consideration: If you're doing some work yourself, assess your skills realistically and allocate time accordingly.

Step 7: Manage the Renovation Process

Supervision: Regularly visit the site to monitor progress and ensure quality.
Communication: Maintain clear and frequent communication with your team.

Additional Resources

Design Software: Utilize home design software to visualize changes before implementation.
Workshops: Attend local DIY workshops for hands-on experience and tips.

Checklist for Renovation Planning

- ☐ Define renovation goals.

- ☐ Complete property assessment.

- ☐ Design a detailed plan.

- ☐ Set and allocate budget.

- ☐ Establish a project timeline.

- ☐ Select and coordinate with your team.

- ☐ Manage and supervise the renovation process.

Final Thoughts Effective planning is the cornerstone of successful house flipping renovations. By thoroughly assessing the property, setting clear goals, and carefully managing resources and timelines, you can ensure a smooth renovation process. This detailed planning helps in enhancing the property's value and appeal, ultimately contributing to a successful house flip.

Stick to a Budget: Keep a Strict Eye on Your Finances

Step 1: Set a Realistic Budget

Initial Assessment: Before starting, assess the overall cost of the project. This includes purchase price, renovation costs, holding costs, and selling expenses. **Contingency Plan**: Always include a contingency budget, ideally 10-20% of your total budget, for unforeseen expenses.

Step 2: Break Down Costs

Detailed Breakdown: List all expected expenses, including materials, labor, permits, and professional fees.

Prioritize: Identify which renovations are essential and which are optional or cosmetic. Focus on changes that add the most value.

Step 3: Secure Financing

Funding Sources: Determine how you'll finance the project — savings, loans, or investors.

Terms and Conditions: Understand the terms of any loans or investment agreements, including interest rates and repayment schedules.

Step 4: Track Every Expense

Record Keeping: Keep detailed records of all expenses, no matter how small. Use budgeting software or spreadsheets for better organization.

Receipts and Invoices: Save all receipts and invoices for future reference and tax purposes.

Step 5: Regularly Review Your Budget

Weekly Check-ins: Schedule regular times to review your budget and expenses. This helps in identifying any overruns early.

Adjust as Needed: Be prepared to make adjustments to stay on track. This might mean delaying or modifying some renovations.

Step 6: Avoid Impulse Spending

Plan Purchases: Make purchasing decisions based on your plan and budget, not on impulse.
Comparison Shop: Look for deals and compare prices before buying materials or hiring contractors.

Step 7: Keep an Eye on the End Goal

Profit Margin: Always keep the potential profit in mind. Overspending can significantly eat into your returns.
ROI Focus: Every decision should be made with the return on investment (ROI) in mind.

Additional Resources

Budgeting Apps: Utilize apps and software designed for budget tracking and project management.
Financial Advisors: Consider consulting a financial advisor for larger projects or investment strategies.

Checklist for Sticking to a Budget

- Set a comprehensive budget.

- Secure and understand your financing.

- Keep meticulous financial records.

- Regularly review and adjust the budget.

- Make cost-effective decisions.

- Focus on ROI with every expense.

Final Thoughts Sticking to a budget in house flipping is crucial for ensuring profitability. It requires discipline, detailed record-keeping, and constant vigilance. By carefully managing your finances throughout the project, you can maximize your return on investment and make your house flipping venture a success.

Understand the Timeframe: Estimate How Long the Project Will Take

Overview: Estimating the timeframe for a house flipping project is crucial for success. A well-planned timeline helps in efficient resource allocation, budget management, and meeting your profit goals. This section provides practical steps to accurately estimate the project duration.

Step-by-Step Guide:

- **Initial Assessment:**

    Inspect the Property: Conduct a thorough inspection to understand the extent of renovations needed.

List Renovation Tasks: Create a comprehensive list of all tasks, from minor repairs to major overhauls.

- **Consult with Professionals:**

  Gather Expert Opinions: Speak with contractors, architects, and other professionals to get realistic time estimates for each task.
  Consider Their Availability: Factor in the schedules of these professionals, as their availability can impact your timeline.

- **Account for Permits and Regulations:**

  Research Local Regulations: Understand the time needed for obtaining permits and adhering to local building codes.
  Include Buffer Time: Always include extra time in your estimates for unexpected delays in this area.

- **Plan for Material Delivery and Labor:**

  Coordinate Supply Chain: Estimate the time for material delivery and ensure it aligns with your renovation schedule.
  Assess Labor Requirements: Determine if you have enough labor to meet your timeline, considering potential delays or workforce shortages.

- **Create a Detailed Timeline:**

  Use Project Management Tools: Leverage software or tools to lay out a detailed, week-by-week or even day-by-day schedule.
  Include Milestones: Set clear milestones for major phases of the project.

- **Review and Adjust:**

  Regularly Reassess: Continuously monitor progress and adjust the timeline as needed.
  Stay Flexible: Be prepared to make changes in response to unforeseen challenges.

Checklist:

- ☐ Complete property inspection.
- ☐ List all renovation tasks.
- ☐ Consult with professionals.
- ☐ Research permits and regulations.
- ☐ Plan for materials and labor.
- ☐ Create a detailed timeline.
- ☐ Regularly reassess and adjust.

Additional Resources:

- Project Management Software: Tools like Asana or Trello can help in tracking progress.
- Contractor Networks: Platforms for finding reliable contractors and understanding their timelines.

Motivational Note: Remember, a well-estimated timeframe is not just about adhering to deadlines; it's about maximizing efficiency and profitability. Your ability to accurately predict and manage time can significantly impact the success of your house flipping project. Stay proactive, adaptable, and always plan with a buffer for the unexpected. Your diligence in time management will pay off in successful, timely project completions.

Advanced Time Management Strategies

- **Leverage Technology for Efficiency:**

    Utilize Construction Management Software: Invest in software that offers real-time tracking of tasks, budgeting, and team communication.
    Adopt Digital Tools for Scheduling: Use digital calendars and scheduling tools to coordinate tasks and deadlines effectively.

- **Implement Agile Methodologies:**

    Adopt an Iterative Approach: Break down the project into smaller, manageable segments, allowing for more flexibility and quicker adjustments.

Regular Stand-up Meetings: Schedule short, daily meetings with your team to assess progress and tackle any immediate issues.

- **Risk Management:**

  Identify Potential Risks: Analyze factors that could cause delays, such as weather conditions, supply chain issues, or labor shortages.
  Develop Contingency Plans: Have backup plans for critical aspects of your project to minimize downtime.

- **Effective Communication:**

  Maintain Open Lines of Communication: Ensure everyone involved, from contractors to suppliers, is on the same page regarding the project's timeline.
  Use Clear, Concise Messaging: Avoid misunderstandings and delays by communicating plans and changes effectively.

Prioritize Tasks:

  Determine Critical Path: Identify tasks that directly impact the project's completion date and prioritize them.
  Focus on High-Impact Activities: Allocate more resources and attention to activities that have the most significant effect on the timeline.

Monitor Progress Regularly:

Track Milestones: Regularly check if the project is meeting set milestones and adjust the plan as necessary.

Use Performance Metrics: Implement key performance indicators (KPIs) to measure progress and identify areas needing improvement.

In house flipping, time is as valuable as money. Mastering the art of accurate time estimation and effective time management can significantly increase your chances of success. Remember, every day saved is a step closer to your profit goal. Stay organized, be proactive, and always be ready to adapt to changes. Your skill in managing time will set you apart in the competitive world of house flipping.

Prioritize Key Improvements: Focus on Renovations That Increase Value

Overview: In house flipping, not all renovations are created equal. Prioritizing key improvements that significantly boost property value is essential for a profitable flip. This section guides you through identifying and focusing on renovations that offer the best return on investment (ROI).

Identifying Value-Adding Renovations:

Market Research: Understand the local real estate market and what buyers in the area value most. This can vary significantly from one neighborhood to another.

High-ROI Areas: Typically, kitchens and bathrooms offer the highest ROI. Upgrading these areas can be a game changer in the overall appeal and value of the property.

Curb Appeal: First impressions matter. Simple exterior improvements like landscaping, painting, and door replacement can dramatically improve a home's curb appeal.

Energy Efficiency: Modern buyers are increasingly environmentally conscious. Investing in energy-efficient windows, insulation, and appliances can be a significant selling point.

Functional Improvements: Addressing any functional issues, such as repairing a leaky roof or updating an old electrical system, is crucial. These improvements might not be immediately visible but are essential for the home's integrity.

Strategic Approach to Renovations:

Budget Allocation: Allocate your budget smartly. Invest more in high-impact areas while keeping other renovations modest and cost-effective.

DIY vs. Professional Help: Evaluate what you can do yourself versus what requires professional skills. Some tasks might seem simple but can significantly impact the property's value when done professionally.

Staging and Finishing Touches: Don't underestimate the power of good staging and finishing touches like modern fixtures, fresh paint, and tasteful landscaping.

Real-World Example: Consider a successful house flip where the investor focused on a complete kitchen remodel, adding a contemporary bathroom, and enhancing the home's curb appeal. These targeted improvements resulted in a significant increase in the property's market value and a quick sale.

Conclusion:

Prioritizing renovations in a house flipping project is more art than science. It requires a keen understanding of the market, a clear vision of the end product, and smart budgeting. By focusing on key improvements that add the most value, you maximize your chances of a profitable flip and reduce the time the property spends on the market. Remember, in the world of house flipping, strategic improvements are the cornerstone of success.

Navigate Legal Requirements: Understand Zoning Laws and Permits

Understanding the Legal Landscape: When embarking on a house flipping project, it's imperative to have a solid grasp of the legal requirements that govern property development. This understanding is critical not only to ensure compliance but also to avoid costly delays and fines that can derail your project. Navigating the complex world of zoning laws and permits can be daunting, but with the right approach, it becomes a manageable part of your flipping process.

Zoning Laws: The Foundation of Property Development
Zoning laws are local regulations that dictate how a property can be used. These laws vary significantly from one area to another, and they can have a profound impact on your

house flipping project. They determine what kind of building can be constructed or altered, the types of activities that can be conducted in a particular area, and the physical parameters of the development, such as building height, density, and the distance from the street.

Key Aspects to Consider:

- **Research Local Zoning Ordinances:** Start by understanding the zoning laws in your project's area. This information is typically available through the local city or county planning department.
- **Impact on Your Project:** Assess how these laws impact your intended renovations. For instance, if you plan to convert a single-family home into a multi-family dwelling, ensure this is permissible under the local zoning laws.
- **Future Zoning Changes:** Stay informed about potential zoning changes. Sometimes, areas are rezoned, which can either positively or negatively impact your project.

Permits: Navigating the Paper Trail Permits are official approvals from local governments to proceed with construction or renovation. They ensure that your project complies with building codes, which cover structural safety, health standards, and environmental regulations.

Navigating Permit Requirements:

- **Identify Necessary Permits:** Different types of work require different permits. For example, structural changes usually need a building permit, while electrical or plumbing work may require specialized permits.

- **Permit Application Process:** Understand the application process in your area. This usually involves submitting detailed plans and undergoing inspections.
- **Timing and Costs:** Factor in the time and cost associated with obtaining permits. Delays in permit approval can extend your project timeline, so plan accordingly.

Legal Compliance: Ensuring a Smooth Project Flow

Staying compliant with zoning laws and permits is not just a legal obligation; it's a strategic approach to house flipping. It prevents interruptions and additional costs associated with non-compliance. It also ensures the safety and habitability of the property, which is crucial for selling the property at a good value.

Building a Network of Experts: Consider building relationships with local experts such as real estate attorneys, experienced contractors, and city officials. They can provide invaluable insights into the legal aspects of house flipping in your area. Their expertise can help streamline the process, from understanding zoning nuances to navigating the permit application process efficiently.

Concluding Thoughts: Understanding and complying with zoning laws and permits is a crucial aspect of house flipping. It requires due diligence, careful planning, and sometimes, patience. However, the effort invested in navigating these legal requirements pays off by ensuring that your project proceeds without legal hurdles, ultimately contributing to its success. Remember, in the world of real estate, being well-versed in legal matters is not just about following rules; it's about making informed decisions that safeguard your investment and maximize your returns.

Develop Negotiation Skills: Hone Your Ability to Negotiate Deals

The Art of Negotiation in House Flipping: Negotiation is a critical skill in the world of house flipping. It's not just about getting the lowest possible price for a property or the best terms from a contractor; it's about creating value, building relationships, and navigating complex deals to ensure profitability. Developing strong negotiation skills can significantly impact your success as a house flipper.

Understanding the Negotiation Landscape: Negotiation in house flipping occurs at various stages, from purchasing the property, dealing with contractors, to selling the renovated house. Each stage requires a different approach and skill set.

A successful negotiator understands the nuances of these different stages and adapts their strategy accordingly.

Strategies for Effective Negotiation:

Preparation is Key: Before entering any negotiation, thorough preparation is essential. This involves understanding the market value of properties, the cost of renovations, and the potential resale value of the house. It also means being aware of the other party's needs and objectives. Preparation gives you the foundation to negotiate from a position of strength.

Building Rapport: Successful negotiation is not just about hard bargaining; it's also about building a relationship with the other party. Establishing rapport can lead to more favorable deals and ongoing business relationships. This involves active listening, showing respect, and understanding the other party's perspective.

Clear Communication: Effective communication is the cornerstone of good negotiation. This means being clear about your objectives, but also being an attentive listener. It's about finding common ground and working towards a solution that benefits all parties involved.

Flexibility and Creativity: Negotiations rarely go exactly as planned. Being flexible and creative in your approach can help navigate through impasses. This might involve offering alternative solutions, adjusting your terms, or finding innovative ways to add value to the deal.

Know When to Walk Away: An essential aspect of negotiation is knowing when to walk away. This comes from understanding your bottom line and being willing to walk away if a deal does not meet your criteria. It's important not to get emotionally attached to a deal, as this can lead to making compromised decisions.

Closing the Deal: A successful negotiation leads to a clear and concise agreement. Ensure all parties understand the terms of the deal and that these are documented in a legally binding contract. This helps prevent misunderstandings and ensures the agreement is honored.

Practicing and Improving Your Skills: Negotiation is a skill that improves with practice. Engage in as many negotiations as possible, even in small deals, to hone your skills. Seek feedback, learn from each experience, and continuously refine your approach. Consider training courses or workshops in negotiation to further enhance your skills.

Conclusion:

Negotiation is a dynamic and vital skill in house flipping. It involves preparation, effective communication, and a deep understanding of the real estate market. By developing and honing your negotiation skills, you position yourself to make better deals, reduce costs, and increase your profitability. Remember, every successful negotiation is a step towards becoming a more effective and profitable house flipper.

Learn to Spot Potential: Identify Homes with Hidden Value

The Essence of Spotting Potential: In the world of house flipping, the ability to spot potential in a property is what separates the successful flippers from the rest. This skill involves looking beyond the apparent flaws and seeing the hidden value in a home. It's about visualizing what a property could become, rather than just what it is at present. This section delves into how to develop this crucial skill and apply it to your house flipping endeavors.

Understanding the Dynamics of Hidden Value: Hidden value in a house can come in many forms. It might be a solid structure beneath an outdated exterior, a great location with poor curb appeal, or unique architectural features overshadowed by neglect. The key is to identify these hidden gems and understand how they can be transformed into profitable assets.

Strategies for Identifying Potential:

Comprehensive Market Knowledge: Gaining an in-depth understanding of the real estate market is vital. This includes knowledge about different neighborhoods, local property values, future development plans, and real estate trends. This information can help you identify areas where properties are undervalued or poised for growth.

Assessing the Property: When evaluating a potential property, it's important to look at it with a critical eye. This involves assessing the structural integrity of the house, the layout, and the potential for improvements. Look for houses that require cosmetic updates rather than extensive structural repairs, as these often provide a better return on investment.

Understanding Renovation Potential: Evaluate what changes can be made to a property and how these changes will affect its value. This might involve adding rooms, updating kitchens and bathrooms, or improving landscaping. The goal is to make improvements that will significantly increase the property's market value.

Cost-Benefit Analysis: Before making a decision, conduct a thorough cost-benefit analysis. Estimate the cost of the required renovations and compare this with the potential increase in property value. Properties that require minimal investment for a substantial increase in value are ideal targets.

Learning from Experience: Experience is a great teacher in house flipping. Each property you assess and work on provides valuable lessons. Take note of what worked and what didn't, and use this knowledge to refine your ability to spot potential.

Networking with Professionals: Building a network of real estate professionals can provide insights into finding properties with hidden value. Real estate agents, contractors, and other flippers can offer valuable tips and alert you to potential deals.

Conclusion:

Learning to spot potential in houses is a blend of art and science. It requires market knowledge, a keen eye for detail, analytical skills, and sometimes, a bit of intuition. By honing this skill, you can identify properties that others overlook and turn them into profitable flips. Remember, the most successful house flippers are those who can see beyond the present condition and envision what a property could become.

Network Effectively: Build Relationships with Real Estate Professionals

The Power of Networking in House Flipping: Networking is a cornerstone of success in the house flipping business. Building a robust network of real estate professionals can open doors to new opportunities, provide valuable insights, and facilitate smoother transactions. This section explores how to network effectively and create lasting relationships in the real estate industry.

Why Networking Matters: The real estate industry is heavily reliant on relationships and connections. A well-connected house flipper can access better deals, get recommendations for reliable contractors, and gain insights into market trends and opportunities. Effective networking can also lead to partnerships, mentorships, and support systems that are invaluable for both new and experienced flippers.

Strategies for Effective Networking:

Attend Industry Events: Participating in real estate conferences, workshops, and local meetups is a great way to meet professionals. These events offer opportunities to connect with realtors, contractors, investors, and other flippers. Be proactive in introducing yourself and engaging in conversations.

Leverage Social Media and Online Platforms: Platforms like LinkedIn, real estate forums, and Facebook groups are excellent for connecting with industry professionals. Join relevant groups, participate in discussions, and share your experiences and knowledge.

Build Genuine Relationships: Networking is not just about exchanging business cards; it's about building genuine relationships. Show interest in others' work, ask questions, and offer help when you can. Remember, effective networking is a two-way street.

Follow-Up and Stay in Touch: After meeting someone, follow up with a message or an email. Express your appreciation for their time and reiterate your interest in staying connected. Regularly check in with your contacts to keep the relationship alive and updated.

Collaborate and Share Opportunities: Look for opportunities to collaborate or share leads with your contacts. This can help strengthen relationships and can lead to mutual benefits in the future.

Seek Mentorship: Networking can also lead to mentorship opportunities. Experienced professionals can provide guidance, advice, and insights that are invaluable for a novice house flipper.

Be a Resource to Others: Offer your knowledge and experience to others. Being helpful and resourceful makes you a valuable member of the network and encourages others to reciprocate.

Conclusion:

Effective networking is about creating and nurturing professional relationships that are beneficial and supportive. In the house flipping industry, these connections can be the key to accessing better deals, gaining valuable advice, and navigating challenges more effectively. Remember, in real estate, your network is one of your most significant assets. Building and maintaining a strong professional network can significantly impact the success and growth of your house flipping venture.

Master the Art of Bargaining: Get the Best Prices for Properties and Materials

The Role of Bargaining in House Flipping:
Bargaining is a critical skill in the house flipping business. It involves negotiating to get the best possible prices for properties and materials, which directly affects the profitability of your projects. Mastering this art can lead to significant cost savings, allowing for a higher return on investment.

Understanding the Bargaining Process: Bargaining in house flipping is not just about getting the lowest price. It's about understanding the value of what you're buying, the market conditions, and the motivations of the other party. Effective bargaining leads to deals that are beneficial for all involved, fostering good relationships with suppliers and sellers, which can be advantageous in the long run.

Strategies for Effective Bargaining:

Do Your Homework: Knowledge is power in negotiations. Research the market value of properties and the standard costs of materials. Understand the current real estate market trends, as these will influence your bargaining power.

Build Rapport with Sellers and Suppliers: Establishing a good relationship with sellers and suppliers can lead to better deals. People are more likely to offer favorable terms to someone they trust and respect.

Communicate Clearly and Confidently: Clearly communicate your offer and be confident in your negotiation. This doesn't mean being aggressive; rather, it's about being assertive and firm in your stance.

Be Willing to Walk Away: One of the most powerful tools in bargaining is the ability to walk away. If the price isn't right, be prepared to leave the negotiation table. This can sometimes lead to the other party reconsidering their stance.

Look for Win-Win Situations: Aim for a deal that benefits both parties. This could mean finding creative ways to structure the deal, such as offering quicker payments in exchange for a lower price.

Use Leverage: If you have something that the other party wants, such as the potential for future business, use it as leverage in your negotiations.

Stay Calm and Patient: Negotiations can be challenging and time-consuming. Stay calm and patient throughout the process. Rushing a deal can lead to suboptimal outcomes.

Practicing Your Bargaining Skills: Like any skill, bargaining gets better with practice. Engage in small negotiations to hone your skills, and learn from each experience. You can also learn from experienced negotiators by observing how they handle negotiations.

Conclusion:

Mastering the art of bargaining is crucial in house flipping. It's about striking the right balance between getting the best price and maintaining good relationships with those you do business with. Effective bargaining leads to reduced costs, increased profitability, and the development of beneficial long-term relationships. Remember, every dollar saved through smart bargaining adds directly to your bottom line.

Understand Tax Implications: Know How Taxes Will Affect Your Profits

Navigating Taxation in House Flipping: Understanding the tax implications associated with house flipping is vital for any real estate investor. Taxes can significantly impact the profitability of your flips, and failure to properly manage tax obligations can lead to unexpected liabilities. This section aims to provide a foundational understanding of the tax considerations in house flipping, helping you to maximize profits and minimize tax burdens.

Key Tax Considerations in House Flipping:

Capital Gains Tax: Profits from house flipping are typically subjected to capital gains tax. The rate can vary based on how long you hold the property. Short-term capital gains (for properties held less than a year) are taxed at a higher rate than long-term gains.

Business Income vs. Capital Gains: The IRS may classify frequent and short-term flipping activities as a business, which means profits could be considered business income, subject to different tax rates and obligations compared to capital gains.

Deductible Expenses: Many expenses related to house flipping are tax-deductible. These can include renovation costs, interest on loans, real estate taxes, and marketing expenses. Keeping detailed records of all expenses is crucial for claiming these deductions.

Depreciation Recapture: If you've claimed depreciation on a property, be aware of depreciation recapture when you sell. This can increase your tax liability.

1031 Exchange: For long-term investments, consider a 1031 exchange, which allows you to defer capital gain taxes by reinvesting the proceeds from a sale into another property.

State and Local Taxes: In addition to federal taxes, be aware of state and local taxes that may apply to your flipping activities.

Self-Employment Taxes: If flipping houses is your primary business, you may be subject to self-employment taxes, which cover Social Security and Medicare taxes.

Seeking Professional Advice: Given the complexities of tax laws, it's advisable to consult with a tax professional who specializes in real estate. They can provide tailored advice and strategies for your specific situation.

Staying Informed and Compliant: Tax laws and regulations can change, so staying informed is crucial. Attend seminars, read up on current tax laws, and keep abreast of any changes that could affect your flipping business.

Conclusion: Understanding and effectively managing tax implications is a critical aspect of house flipping. Proper tax planning can help you retain more of your profits and avoid legal complications. Always prioritize compliance with tax laws and seek professional advice to navigate the complex tax landscape of real estate investing. With the right approach, you can make informed decisions that positively influence the financial outcome of your flips.

Stay Informed on Market Changes: Keep Up with Real Estate Trends

The Importance of Market Awareness: In the fast-paced world of real estate, market conditions can change rapidly. For house flippers, staying informed about these changes is crucial. Understanding current trends, economic factors, and consumer preferences can significantly impact the success of your investments. This section explores how to effectively stay abreast of real estate market changes and use this knowledge to make informed decisions.

Staying Ahead of the Curve:

Regularly Monitor Market Data: Keep an eye on real estate market data, including housing prices, inventory levels, interest rates, and economic indicators. This data provides valuable insights into market trends and can help you anticipate future changes.

Understand Local Dynamics: Real estate markets can vary greatly from one area to another. It's important to understand the specifics of the markets where you are investing, including neighborhood trends, local economic conditions, and development plans.

Follow Industry News and Publications: Stay informed by reading real estate news, subscribing to industry publications, and following reputable real estate websites and blogs. This will keep you updated on national trends, new legislation, and emerging market opportunities.

Leverage Technology and Tools: Utilize technology and online tools to gather and analyze market data. Real estate analytics platforms can provide comprehensive insights into market trends and forecasts.

Network with Industry Professionals: Building a network of real estate agents, brokers, and other investors can provide first-hand market insights. These professionals can offer valuable perspectives based on their on-the-ground experiences.

Attend Real Estate Seminars and Events: Participate in real estate seminars, webinars, and conferences. These events are great opportunities to learn from experts and discuss market trends with other investors.

Adapt to Market Changes: Be prepared to adjust your investment strategies in response to market shifts. Flexibility and adaptability are key to capitalizing on new opportunities and mitigating risks.

Utilizing Market Knowledge: Use your understanding of market trends to make strategic decisions about property acquisitions, renovations, and sales. For example, if there's a growing trend for sustainable living, consider eco-friendly renovations to appeal to environmentally conscious buyers.

Conclusion:

Staying informed about real estate market changes is not just about reacting to current conditions; it's about anticipating future trends and positioning yourself accordingly. By maintaining a deep understanding of market dynamics, you can make more informed decisions, reduce risks, and increase the likelihood of success in your house flipping ventures. Remember, in real estate, knowledge is not just power—it's profit.

Manage Risks: Identify and Mitigate Potential Risks

The Necessity of Risk Management in House Flipping:
Risk management is an essential aspect of house flipping. Identifying and mitigating potential risks can mean the difference between a profitable flip and a financial loss. This section explores the various types of risks associated with house flipping and provides strategies for effectively managing them.

Understanding the Risks:

Market Risks: Market fluctuations can significantly impact the value of real estate. Economic downturns, changes in interest rates, and shifts in consumer preferences can all affect the profitability of a flip.

Financial Risks: Overestimating the property's after-repair value (ARV) or underestimating the renovation costs can lead to financial strain. Additionally, unexpected expenses, such as hidden structural issues, can increase costs.

Legal and Compliance Risks: Failure to comply with building codes, zoning laws, or permit requirements can result in fines and delays. It's important to be aware of and adhere to all legal requirements.

Contractor Risks: Working with unreliable or unqualified contractors can lead to subpar work, delays, and additional costs. Thorough vetting and clear contracts are essential.

Strategies for Risk Management:

Conduct Thorough Due Diligence: Before purchasing a property, conduct a comprehensive evaluation, including a detailed inspection and market analysis. Understand the property's condition and the local real estate market.

Develop a Realistic Budget and Timeline: Create a detailed budget and timeline that includes a buffer for unexpected expenses and delays. This helps in managing financial risks effectively.

Stay Informed and Adaptable: Keep abreast of market trends and economic indicators. Be prepared to adjust your strategies in response to market changes.

Reliable Team: Work with experienced and reputable professionals, including real estate agents, contractors, and legal advisors. A strong team can help mitigate various risks.

Secure Adequate Insurance: Ensure you have appropriate insurance coverage for the property during the renovation process. This can protect against accidents, theft, and other unforeseen events.

Legal Compliance: Ensure all renovations are compliant with local laws and regulations. Obtain necessary permits and have work inspected to avoid legal complications.

Learning from Experience: Each house flipping project offers valuable lessons in risk management. Analyze the outcomes of your projects, identify what worked and what didn't, and use this knowledge to improve your risk management strategies in future projects.

Conclusion:

Effective risk management is crucial for the success of house flipping projects. By identifying and proactively addressing potential risks, you can minimize negative impacts and maximize your chances of achieving a profitable outcome. Remember, in real estate investing, being prepared for and responsive to risks is just as important as identifying opportunities.

Leverage Technology: Use Real Estate and Project Management Software

Embracing Technology in House Flipping: In the modern world of house flipping, technology plays a pivotal role. Leveraging technology through real estate and project management software can streamline processes, enhance efficiency, and lead to more informed decision-making. This section delves into the various technological tools available to house flippers and how they can be effectively utilized.

The Benefits of Technology in Real Estate Investing:

Improved Market Analysis: Real estate software provides access to comprehensive market data, including listings, historical price trends, and demographic information. This data is crucial for identifying profitable investment opportunities and understanding market dynamics.

Efficient Project Management: Project management tools allow for the effective organization and tracking of renovation projects. They can help in scheduling, budgeting, communicating with team members, and monitoring progress.

Enhanced Property Visualization: Technologies like virtual reality (VR) and 3D modeling provide advanced ways to visualize properties and potential renovations. This can be a powerful tool for planning and marketing.

Streamlined Communication: Communication tools integrated into project management software facilitate better coordination with contractors, real estate agents, and other stakeholders.

Document Management and Organization: Keeping digital records of contracts, invoices, permits, and other documents reduces paperwork and improves organization.

Types of Technology to Leverage:

Real Estate Investment Software: Platforms that offer market analysis, property valuation, and investment projections.

Project Management Software: Tools like Trello, Asana, or specialized construction management software to manage renovation timelines and budgets.

Virtual Reality and 3D Modeling: Technologies for visualizing renovations and staging properties virtually, enhancing the marketing and planning process.

Customer Relationship Management (CRM) Software: For managing interactions with clients, contractors, and other professionals.

Financial Management Tools: Software for budget tracking, expense management, and financial forecasting.

Conclusion:

Incorporating technology into your house flipping business is not just about staying current; it's about gaining a competitive edge. By leveraging the right technological tools, you can optimize your operations, make data-driven decisions, and ultimately achieve greater success in your real estate investments. In an industry as dynamic as real estate, staying technologically savvy is key to staying ahead.

Cultivate Patience: Understand That Good Deals Take Time

The Virtue of Patience in House Flipping: In the high-energy world of house flipping, patience is often an undervalued yet crucial trait. The ability to wait for the right opportunity and not rush into decisions can significantly influence the success of your real estate ventures. This section discusses the importance of cultivating patience in finding profitable deals, managing renovations, and navigating the real estate market.

Why Patience Matters:

Finding the Right Property: The best deals in house flipping are often the ones that take time to find. Patience is key when searching for properties that offer the right balance of price, location, and potential for value addition.

Waiting for Market Conditions: Real estate markets fluctuate. Sometimes, the wisest decision is to wait for the right market conditions before selling a flipped property to maximize profit.

Dealing with Renovation Delays: Renovations rarely go exactly as planned. Patience is essential when dealing with unexpected delays and challenges that arise during the renovation process.

Cultivating Patience in Your Business:

Set Realistic Expectations: Understand that house flipping is not a get-rich-quick scheme. Set realistic expectations about the time required to find, renovate, and sell properties.

Develop a Strategic Approach: Instead of rushing into deals, take the time to develop a strategic approach. Analyze each potential investment thoroughly to ensure it aligns with your business goals.

Build a Buffer into Your Plans: When planning timelines and budgets, build in buffers for unexpected delays and expenses. This reduces stress and pressure, allowing you to make more considered decisions.

Practice Mindful Decision-Making: Make decisions based on thorough research and analysis, rather than impulsive reactions. Mindful decision-making often leads to more profitable outcomes.

Learn from Experience: Use experiences from past projects to cultivate patience. Reflect on instances where a patient approach led to success or where impatience resulted in missed opportunities.

Embracing Patience as a Business Philosophy: Incorporate patience into your business philosophy. Recognize that some of the best opportunities emerge from a patient, disciplined approach. Patience can become a competitive advantage, allowing you to capitalize on opportunities that others may overlook due to haste.

Conclusion:

Cultivating patience in house flipping is about more than just waiting; it's about making informed, strategic decisions that lead to successful outcomes. By embracing patience, you can navigate the complexities of real estate investing with a clearer perspective, leading to more consistent and profitable results. In the fast-paced world of house flipping, sometimes the best action is calculated patience.

Maintain High Standards: Ensure Quality in All Renovations

The Imperative of Quality in House Flipping: In house flipping, the quality of your renovations can significantly impact the success of your project. High standards in renovations not only increase the property's value but also build your reputation as a quality house flipper. This section emphasizes the importance of maintaining high standards and ensuring quality in every aspect of your renovations.

Why Quality Matters:

Attracting Buyers: High-quality renovations attract buyers and can command higher prices. Attention to detail and quality craftsmanship make properties stand out in a competitive market.

Long-Term Value: Quality renovations contribute to the long-term value and durability of the property, reducing the likelihood of future issues and complaints from buyers.

Reputation: Your reputation as a house flipper is tied to the quality of your work. Consistently high standards lead to positive reviews, referrals, and repeat business.

Strategies for Ensuring Quality:

Select the Right Contractors: Work with reliable and skilled contractors known for their quality work. Vet their previous projects and check references before hiring.

Use Quality Materials: Invest in high-quality materials that offer durability and aesthetic appeal. While they may cost more upfront, they pay off in the long run by enhancing the property's value and appeal.

Focus on Key Areas: Prioritize areas that have the most significant impact on buyers, such as kitchens and bathrooms. High-quality work in these areas can significantly boost the property's appeal.

Regular Inspections: Conduct regular inspections throughout the renovation process to ensure that work meets your standards. Address any issues promptly to maintain quality.

Stay Informed on Trends: Keep up with current design trends and technologies. Incorporating modern, popular elements can enhance the property's appeal and functionality.

Attention to Detail: Pay attention to the small details, as they can make a big difference in the overall perception of quality. This includes aspects like neat paint edges, properly installed fixtures, and well-finished carpentry.

The Impact of Quality on Profitability: Quality renovations may require more time and investment, but they can lead to higher profits. Properties that are well-renovated tend to sell faster and at higher prices, maximizing your return on investment.

Conclusion:

Maintaining high standards in renovations is crucial for the success of your house flipping business. It not only leads to higher property values and quicker sales but also builds your reputation as a quality flipper. In the real estate market, where competition is fierce, the quality of your work can set you apart and pave the way for long-term success. Remember, in house flipping, quality is not an expense; it's an investment in your business's future.

Balance Speed and Quality: Work Efficiently Without Sacrificing Quality

Striking the Right Balance: In house flipping, time is money, but quality is king. The challenge lies in balancing the need for speed in completing renovations with the imperative of maintaining high quality. This balance is crucial for maximizing profitability while building a reputation for excellence. This section focuses on how to achieve this balance, ensuring that your renovations are both time-efficient and of high quality.

Why Balancing Speed and Quality Matters:

Market Advantage: Properties that are renovated quickly and to a high standard are more likely to sell faster and at a better price, giving you a competitive edge in the market.

Cost Efficiency: Efficient work processes can reduce labor costs and minimize holding costs, such as interest payments and utilities.

Reputation: A balance of speed and quality enhances your reputation as a reliable and skilled house flipper, leading to potential referrals and repeat business

How to Achieve the Balance:

Efficient Planning and Scheduling: Before starting the renovation, create a detailed plan and schedule. Efficient planning helps in identifying potential bottlenecks and allows for smoother execution of tasks.

Hiring Skilled Professionals: Work with contractors and tradespeople who are skilled and experienced. They are more likely to understand the importance of this balance and can work efficiently without compromising on quality.

Using the Right Tools and Materials: Invest in high-quality materials and the right tools. Quality materials contribute to the overall finish of the project, and the right tools can significantly increase efficiency.

Regular Monitoring and Quality Checks: Regularly monitor the progress of the renovation and perform quality checks at different stages. This helps in catching and correcting any issues early, preventing costly rework.

Effective Communication: Maintain clear and continuous communication with your team. This ensures that everyone is aligned with the project goals and can quickly address any issues that arise.

Leveraging Technology: Use project management software to track progress, manage tasks, and maintain schedules. Technology can greatly enhance efficiency in project management.

Conclusion:

Balancing speed and quality in house flipping is a delicate yet achievable task. It requires thoughtful planning, collaboration with skilled professionals, and a commitment to excellence. By mastering this balance, you can enhance the profitability of your projects, reduce risks, and build a strong reputation in the competitive world of real estate investing. Remember, in house flipping, efficiency and quality are not mutually exclusive; they are complementary elements of a successful project.

Adapt to Challenges: Be Ready to Tackle Unforeseen Problems

The Reality of Unforeseen Challenges: House flipping, like any real estate venture, is full of unpredictability. Projects often encounter unforeseen challenges ranging from structural issues to budget overruns. The ability to adapt to these challenges is crucial for the success of a flipping project. This section focuses on strategies to effectively tackle unexpected problems and maintain the course towards a successful flip.

Why Adaptability is Key:

Problem-Solving: Adaptability is essential for solving the unique and unexpected problems that arise during renovations. It involves finding creative and practical solutions to keep the project on track.

Risk Management: Being adaptable helps in managing risks effectively. It allows you to adjust your plans and strategies in response to unexpected situations, thereby minimizing potential losses.

Meeting Deadlines: Adaptable strategies can help in meeting project deadlines despite setbacks, ensuring that the property can be put on the market as planned.

How to Cultivate Adaptability:

Expect the Unexpected: Approach each project with the understanding that unforeseen issues are likely to arise. This mindset prepares you to handle surprises without undue stress.

Build a Flexible Plan: While detailed planning is important, ensure that your plans have the flexibility to accommodate changes. This could involve having contingency budgets or alternative timelines.

Stay Informed and Educated: Continuously educate yourself about various aspects of house flipping. The more knowledgeable you are, the better equipped you'll be to handle unexpected challenges.

Develop a Strong Network: Having a network of reliable contractors, suppliers, and other real estate professionals can provide crucial support in addressing unforeseen problems.

Leverage Technology: Utilize project management and problem-solving tools that can help you adjust plans and communicate changes quickly and efficiently.

Maintain a Positive Attitude: A positive mindset is vital in adapting to challenges. Viewing problems as opportunities to learn and grow can transform your approach to handling them.

Conclusion:

Adaptability in house flipping is about being prepared for the unexpected and having the resilience to navigate through challenges. It involves flexibility, creativity, and a positive approach to problem-solving. By cultivating adaptability, you can ensure that your house flipping projects are resilient to setbacks and positioned for success. Remember, the ability to adapt is not just a skill; it's a mindset that can drive your flipping business towards long-term success and sustainability.

Focus on Curb Appeal: Improve the Property's Exterior Attractiveness

The Significance of Curb Appeal in House Flipping: Curb appeal plays a critical role in house flipping. It's the first impression that a property makes on potential buyers and can significantly influence their perception of the home. Improving a property's exterior attractiveness not only enhances its appeal but can also increase its market value. This section explores effective strategies to boost curb appeal in house flipping projects.

Why Curb Appeal Matters:

First Impressions: The exterior of the property is the first thing potential buyers see, and it sets the tone for their overall impression of the home.

Increased Property Value: Properties with high curb appeal tend to sell at higher prices, as they attract more interest from buyers.

Quick Sales: A property with excellent curb appeal is more likely to sell quickly, reducing the time it spends on the market.

Strategies to Enhance Curb Appeal:

Landscaping: Well-maintained landscaping can dramatically improve the property's appearance. This includes manicured lawns, trimmed hedges, and vibrant flower beds.

Fresh Exterior Paint: A fresh coat of paint can revitalize the exterior of a house. Choose colors that are appealing and complement the style of the property.

Front Door Makeover: The front door is a focal point of curb appeal. Consider painting the door in an inviting color or replacing it with a more stylish option.

Upgrade Lighting: Good outdoor lighting can enhance the property's appearance, especially in the evenings. Stylish light fixtures can also add character to the home.

Clean and Repair: Ensure that the exterior is clean and well-maintained. Repair any visible damage, such as cracked sidewalks or loose siding.

Add Decorative Elements: Small details like house numbers, mailboxes, and door hardware can make a big difference in the property's curb appeal.

Create an Inviting Entryway: An attractive entryway can make the home feel welcoming. Consider adding potted plants, a welcome mat, or seating.

The Impact of Curb Appeal on Marketing: Curb appeal is not just about aesthetics; it's a powerful marketing tool. High-quality exterior photographs can attract more online viewers and drive traffic to property showings.

Conclusion:

Investing in curb appeal is a smart strategy in house flipping. It enhances the property's attractiveness, increases its value, and can lead to quicker sales. Remember, the exterior of your property is a reflection of the overall quality of your renovation, so giving it the attention it deserves can pay significant dividends. In the world of house flipping, a strong curb appeal is an essential ingredient for success.

Maximize Space Utilization: Create a Sense of More Space

The Importance of Space Utilization in House Flipping: In house flipping, how you utilize space can significantly impact the appeal and functionality of a property. Especially in smaller homes, creating a sense of more space can make the property more attractive to potential buyers. This section explores creative strategies to maximize space utilization, transforming cramped areas into open, inviting spaces.

Why Space Utilization is Crucial:

Enhanced Appeal: Efficiently utilized spaces appear larger, more functional, and more inviting, which enhances the property's overall appeal.

Increased Functionality: Smart space utilization improves the functionality of a home, making it more practical and comfortable for living.

Targeting a Wider Market: Maximizing space appeals to a broader range of buyers, including small families, couples, and professionals looking for efficient living spaces.

Strategies for Maximizing Space:

Use Light and Bright Colors: Painting walls in light colors can make rooms appear larger and more open. Bright and neutral colors reflect light better, enhancing the sense of space.

Incorporate Mirrors: Mirrors can create an illusion of more space by reflecting light and views. Strategically placed mirrors can significantly open up a room.

Choose Space-Saving Furniture: Opt for furniture that is proportionate to the room size and offers storage solutions. Multi-functional furniture, like ottomans with storage or Murphy beds, can be particularly effective.
Implement Clever Storage Solutions: Utilize smart storage options to reduce clutter. This includes built-in shelves, under-stair storage, and customized closet systems.

Optimize Room Layout: Arrange furniture and design layouts to maximize open space and improve flow. Avoid blocking pathways and consider the scale and placement of each piece.

Enhance Natural Light: Maximize natural light through the use of large windows, skylights, and open floor plans. Natural light makes spaces feel more airy and spacious.

Use Minimalistic Decor: A minimalistic approach to decor can prevent a space from feeling crowded. Choose a few statement pieces instead of many small decorations.

The Impact on Resale Value: Properties that feel spacious and well-organized tend to have a higher resale value. These homes attract buyers looking for ready-to-move-in properties that require minimal changes.

Conclusion: Maximizing space utilization is key to enhancing the appeal and functionality of a property in house flipping. By implementing creative design strategies, you can transform small or cramped spaces into areas that feel open and welcoming. This not only makes the property more attractive to potential buyers but also can significantly increase its market value. In the realm of house flipping, effective space utilization is not just about maximizing physical space; it's about creating an environment that feels both expansive and intimate.

Stay Organized: Keep All Project Details and Documents Well-Organized

The Importance of Organization in House Flipping:
Organization is a key component of successful house flipping. Keeping all project details, documents, and schedules well-organized can significantly enhance efficiency and reduce the likelihood of errors or oversights. This section discusses the benefits of staying organized in house flipping and provides tips on how to effectively manage project information.

Benefits of Being Organized:

Efficient Project Management: Organization enables more efficient management of the renovation process, from planning to execution.

Time and Cost Savings: Having all information organized and easily accessible saves time and helps in keeping the project within budget.

Improved Communication: Well-organized information facilitates clearer communication with contractors, real estate agents, and other stakeholders.

Compliance and Record-Keeping: Keeping documents organized is crucial for compliance with legal requirements and for maintaining a clear record of the project.

Strategies for Staying Organized:

Use Project Management Tools: Leverage digital project management tools to track progress, manage tasks, and keep documents organized. Tools like Trello, Asana, or specialized real estate software can be invaluable.

Maintain Detailed Records: Keep detailed records of all aspects of the project, including budgets, timelines, contracts, permits, receipts, and correspondence.

Implement a Filing System: Establish a clear and consistent filing system, whether digital or physical, for all project-related documents.

Regular Updates and Reviews: Regularly update and review project information to ensure everything is on track and any changes are recorded.

Use Checklists: Create checklists for different stages of the project to ensure all necessary steps are taken and nothing is overlooked.

Schedule Regular Meetings: Hold regular meetings with your team to review progress and organize upcoming tasks. This keeps everyone aligned and informed.

Leveraging Technology for Organization: Utilize technology to enhance organization. Digital platforms can store, categorize, and provide easy access to all project-related information. They also facilitate sharing and collaboration among team members.

Conclusion:

Staying organized is crucial in house flipping. It streamlines the renovation process, ensures effective communication, and helps in maintaining control over the project. By implementing effective organizational strategies, you can enhance your efficiency and effectiveness as a house flipper, leading to more successful and profitable projects. Remember, in the complex and fast-paced world of house flipping, organization is not just a skill—it's a necessity for success.

Communicate Effectively: Keep Open Lines of Communication with Your Team

The Essence of Effective Communication in House Flipping: Effective communication is fundamental in the world of house flipping. It is key to coordinating efforts, solving problems, and ensuring that everyone involved in the project is on the same page. This section discusses the importance of maintaining open lines of communication with your team and offers strategies for effective communication.

Why Communication Matters:

Enhanced Team Coordination: Effective communication ensures that all team members, including contractors, designers, and real estate agents, are well-coordinated.

Efficient Problem-Solving: Open lines of communication allow for quick identification and resolution of issues, minimizing delays and misunderstandings.

Building Strong Relationships: Good communication builds trust and strengthens relationships with team members, which is essential for long-term success.

Strategies for Effective Communication:

Regular Meetings and Updates: Schedule regular meetings to discuss progress, challenges, and next steps. Frequent updates keep everyone informed and engaged.

Use of Technology: Leverage technology such as messaging apps, email, and project management software for continuous and clear communication.

Clarity and Conciseness: Communicate information clearly and concisely to avoid misunderstandings. Be specific about tasks, deadlines, and expectations.

Encourage Feedback: Create an environment where team members feel comfortable providing feedback. This can lead to valuable insights and ideas.

Active Listening: Effective communication is not just about conveying information, but also about listening. Pay attention to what team members say and address their concerns.

Conflict Resolution: Be prepared to address and resolve conflicts constructively. Open communication is key to finding solutions and maintaining team harmony.

Leveraging Communication for Project Success: Effective communication contributes significantly to the smooth execution and success of house flipping projects. It helps in managing the complexities and dynamic nature of renovation projects.

Conclusion:

In house flipping, effective communication is as important as any technical skill. It enhances teamwork, aids in problem-solving, and drives the project towards its goals. By fostering open and clear communication, you can create a more efficient, collaborative, and successful flipping experience. Remember, good communication is the foundation upon which successful projects are built.

Embrace Sustainability: Consider Eco-Friendly Renovation Options

The Growing Importance of Sustainability in House Flipping: Sustainability is becoming increasingly important in the real estate sector, including house flipping. Eco-friendly renovations not only benefit the environment but also appeal to a growing segment of environmentally conscious buyers. This section explores how to incorporate sustainability into your house flipping projects and the benefits of doing so.

Why Sustainability Matters:

Environmental Impact: Sustainable renovations help in reducing the environmental impact of housing by using eco-friendly materials and reducing energy consumption.

Market Appeal: Eco-friendly homes are becoming more appealing to buyers who are conscious of their environmental footprint and energy costs.

Long-Term Savings: Sustainable features like solar panels and energy-efficient appliances can offer long-term cost savings, making properties more attractive to buyers.

Strategies for Sustainable Renovations:

Energy Efficiency: Incorporate energy-efficient features such as LED lighting, energy-efficient appliances, and proper insulation.

Use of Sustainable Materials: Opt for sustainable and recycled materials in renovations. This can include reclaimed wood, recycled glass, and low-VOC (Volatile Organic Compounds) paints.

Water Conservation: Install water-efficient fixtures like low-flow toilets and showerheads. Consider rainwater harvesting systems for garden use.

Solar Energy: Installing solar panels can significantly reduce energy costs and appeal to environmentally conscious buyers.

Sustainable Landscaping: Implement landscaping that requires minimal water and maintenance. Use native plants and create spaces that complement the local ecosystem.

Smart Home Technology: Smart home technologies can enhance energy efficiency. This includes programmable thermostats, automated lighting systems, and energy monitors.

The Benefits of Embracing Sustainability: Sustainable house flipping can lead to higher property values, a unique selling point in the market, and a positive impact on the environment. It aligns your business with future trends in real estate and demonstrates a commitment to responsible practices.

Conclusion:

Embracing sustainability in house flipping is a forward-thinking approach that aligns with evolving market preferences and environmental concerns. By incorporating eco-friendly renovation options, you can create homes that are not only aesthetically appealing and functional but also environmentally responsible. In the world of real estate investing, sustainability is not just a trend; it's a pathway to creating value for both the property and the planet.

Understand Financing Options: Know Different Lending and Mortgage Avenues

The Role of Financing in House Flipping: Financing is a critical element in the house flipping process. Understanding the various lending and mortgage options available can significantly impact the feasibility and profitability of your projects. This section aims to provide insight into the different financing avenues for house flippers and the importance of choosing the right option for your needs.

Why Understanding Financing is Crucial:

Access to Capital: Knowing your financing options provides access to the capital needed to purchase and renovate properties.

Cost-Effectiveness: Different financing options come with varying costs, interest rates, and terms. Selecting the most cost-effective option can greatly affect your bottom line.

Risk Management: Understanding the risks associated with different types of loans can help you manage and mitigate financial risks.

Types of Financing for House Flipping:

Traditional Mortgages: While not commonly used for flipping due to longer processing times and stricter requirements, traditional mortgages can be an option for longer-term investments.

Hard Money Loans: These are short-term loans from private lenders, ideal for flips due to their quick approval times. However, they often come with higher interest rates.

Private Money Loans: Obtained from individual investors, these loans offer more flexible terms and can be a good option for flippers with strong investor networks.

Home Equity Lines of Credit (HELOCs): For those with existing property, a HELOC can provide a flexible source of funds based on the equity in your property.

Bridge Loans: These are short-term loans used to bridge the gap between buying a new property and selling an existing one.

Cash-Out Refinance: This involves refinancing an existing mortgage and taking out additional cash against the equity in your property.

Strategies for Choosing the Right Financing:

Assess Your Financial Situation: Understand your financial position, credit score, and investment goals to determine the best financing option.

Compare Loan Terms and Rates: Research and compare different lenders' terms, interest rates, and fees to find the most advantageous deal.

Seek Professional Advice: Consult with financial advisors or mortgage brokers who can provide insights and recommendations based on your specific needs.

Understand the Risks: Be aware of the risks associated with each type of financing, including the potential for higher costs and the loss of collateral.

Conclusion:

Understanding the various financing options available is essential for successful house flipping. It allows you to secure the necessary funds while managing costs and risks. Choosing the right financing option can be the difference between a profitable flip and a financial misstep. Remember, in house flipping, informed financing decisions are as important as finding the perfect property to flip.

Be Prepared for Surprises: Set Aside a Contingency Budget

The Inevitability of Surprises in House Flipping: House flipping often comes with its share of surprises, especially during renovations. These unexpected challenges can range from hidden structural issues to unplanned repairs. Being financially prepared for these surprises is crucial. This section discusses the importance of having a contingency budget in place and how it can help manage unforeseen expenses in house flipping projects.

Why a Contingency Budget is Essential:

Financial Safety Net: A contingency budget acts as a financial safety net, providing funds to cover unexpected costs without derailing the overall budget.

Stress Reduction: Knowing you have a financial cushion can reduce stress and allow for more flexibility in handling surprises.

Project Continuity: With a contingency budget, you can address unforeseen issues promptly, keeping the project on track and avoiding delays.

Creating and Managing a Contingency Budget:

Determine the Budget Size: Typically, a contingency budget should be around 10-20% of the total renovation budget. The exact amount can vary depending on the property's condition and the project's complexity.

Separate from Main Budget: Keep the contingency funds separate from your main budget to avoid the temptation of using them for planned expenses.

Prioritize Use of Funds: Use the contingency budget for truly unexpected expenses, not for upgrades or changes that could be considered scope creep.

Regular Budget Reviews: Regularly review and adjust your budgets as the project progresses. If you haven't used your contingency budget near the project's end, you can consider additional upgrades or simply enjoy the higher profits.
Documentation: Document all expenses from the contingency fund. This helps in tracking how the funds are used and in learning for future projects.

The Impact on Project Success: Having a well-planned contingency budget can be the difference between a successful flip and a financial shortfall. It allows you to handle surprises efficiently, ensuring that these unexpected issues don't compromise the quality or profitability of your project.

Conclusion:

Surprises are a natural part of the house flipping process, and being financially prepared for them is essential. A contingency budget is not just a financial tool; it's a strategic element of project planning. It ensures that you are prepared for the unexpected, enabling you to navigate challenges confidently and keep your project moving towards success. Remember, in house flipping, it's not just about expecting the unexpected but also being prepared for it.

Know When to Walk Away: Recognize a Bad Investment Before It's Too Late

The Wisdom of Walking Away: In house flipping, not every potential investment is a good one. Recognizing when to walk away from a property that poses too many risks or requires too much investment is crucial. This section discusses the importance of identifying bad investments and the factors that indicate when it's time to walk away.

Recognizing a Bad Investment:

Excessive Renovation Costs: If the cost of necessary renovations significantly outweighs the potential return on investment, the property may not be viable.

Structural Issues: Major structural problems can be costly to fix and may not be worth the investment.

Legal and Zoning Issues: Properties with legal complications or zoning restrictions can lead to unforeseen expenses and delays.

Market Conditions: Poor market conditions or a declining neighborhood can impact the potential resale value of a property.

Strategies for Evaluating Investments:

Conduct Thorough Due Diligence: Before purchasing a property, conduct a comprehensive inspection and analysis to understand all potential risks and costs.

Consult with Professionals: Seek advice from experienced contractors, real estate agents, and legal professionals to gain a complete picture of the property's potential.

Set Clear Criteria: Define clear criteria for your investments, including budget limits, desired return on investment, and acceptable levels of risk.

Listen to Your Instincts: Sometimes, your instincts can alert you to potential problems. If a deal feels wrong, it's worth taking a step back to reevaluate.

Have an Exit Strategy: Always have a plan for how you can exit the investment if things don't go as planned.

Avoid Emotional Decisions: Avoid getting emotionally attached to a property. Focus on the numbers and the feasibility of the project.

The Benefits of Prudent Decision-Making: Knowing when to walk away can save you from significant financial losses and stress. It ensures that your resources and efforts are directed towards projects with a higher chance of success.

Conclusion:

In house flipping, knowing when to walk away from a bad investment is as important as recognizing a good one. It's a skill that involves careful analysis, consultation with experts, and sometimes, the courage to say no to a seemingly tempting opportunity. Remember, the goal is to make profitable investments, and sometimes the best decision for your business's health and your peace of mind is to walk away.

Enhance Interior Appeal: Focus on Key Interior Improvements

The Impact of Interior Appeal in House Flipping:
Enhancing the interior appeal of a property is crucial in house flipping. It's not just about making a space look attractive; it's about transforming it into a place where potential buyers can envision themselves living. Focusing on key interior improvements can significantly increase a property's value and attractiveness. This section delves into the strategies for enhancing the interior appeal of your flip properties.

Why Interior Appeal Matters:

First Impressions: The interior of the house is often what makes the first and most lasting impression on potential buyers.

Increased Property Value: Well-executed interior improvements can considerably increase the market value of a property.

Broader Market Appeal: Aesthetically pleasing and functional interiors appeal to a wider range of buyers.

Key Strategies for Interior Enhancements:

Modern and Neutral Color Scheme: Use modern, neutral colors for walls and finishes. This appeals to a wider audience and allows potential buyers to easily personalize the space.

Update Kitchen and Bathrooms: Focus on the kitchen and bathrooms, as these areas significantly influence buyers' decisions. Modern appliances, functional layouts, and high-quality finishes are key.

Quality Lighting: Install quality lighting fixtures to enhance the ambiance of the space. Good lighting can make rooms feel more spacious and welcoming.

Maximize Space Utilization: Create a sense of openness and flow. Use space-saving solutions and smart layouts to make the interiors feel more spacious.

Focus on Flooring: Invest in good quality flooring. Hardwood floors or high-quality tiles can significantly enhance the look and feel of a property.

Attention to Detail: Pay attention to the details, such as door handles, crown moldings, and window treatments. These small elements can add a touch of luxury and completeness to the property.

Staging the Property: Professionally stage the property to showcase its potential. Well-placed furniture and decor can help buyers visualize the space as their future home.

The Role of Interior Appeal in Marketing: Beautifully designed interiors are not only appealing during showings but also in marketing materials. High-quality interior photos can attract more online viewers and drive traffic to property showings.

Conclusion:

Enhancing the interior appeal is essential in the house flipping process. It involves thoughtful design, quality improvements, and attention to detail. By focusing on key interior enhancements, you can create a space that not only looks appealing but also feels like a desirable home. In the competitive world of house flipping, a property with a high interior appeal can stand out in the market, ensuring quicker sales and higher returns on your investment.

Invest in Landscaping: Boost Property Value Through Outdoor Aesthetics

The Value of Landscaping in House Flipping: Investing in landscaping is a powerful way to enhance a property's curb appeal and increase its value. Well-designed outdoor spaces can transform a property's appearance, making it more attractive to potential buyers. This section discusses the importance of landscaping in house flipping and how it can be leveraged to boost property value.

Why Landscaping Is Crucial:

Enhanced Curb Appeal: A well-landscaped property creates a strong first impression, significantly improving its curb appeal.

Increased Property Value: Landscaping can increase a property's value. Studies have shown that good landscaping can add up to 10-15% to the value of a home.

Emotional Appeal: Beautiful outdoor spaces can evoke an emotional response from potential buyers, making the property more desirable.

Strategies for Effective Landscaping:

Plan for Aesthetic and Functionality: Design landscaping that is not only aesthetically pleasing but also functional. Consider elements like patios, decks, and garden areas that enhance the living experience.

Use of Native Plants: Incorporate native plants in your landscaping. They are easier to maintain, environmentally friendly, and better adapted to the local climate.

Create an Inviting Entrance: The entrance and walkway are focal points. Use plants, lighting, and hardscaping to create a welcoming entrance.

Add Color and Texture: Use a variety of plants to add color and texture to the landscape. Seasonal flowers, perennial plants, and shrubs can add interest and depth.

Implement Efficient Irrigation: An efficient irrigation system, such as drip irrigation, can be a selling point, ensuring that the landscape remains lush with minimal water waste.

Lighting: Outdoor lighting can transform a property at night, highlighting landscaping features and improving security.

Regular Maintenance: Ensure that the landscaping is well-maintained, especially when the property is on the market.

The Impact of Landscaping on Sales: Properties with well-executed landscaping tend to sell faster. They stand out in listings and are more likely to draw potential buyers for viewings.

Conclusion:

Investing in landscaping is a strategic decision in house flipping that can lead to substantial returns. It not only enhances the visual appeal of a property but also contributes to its overall marketability. A well-landscaped property can be a key differentiator in a competitive market, making it an essential component of successful house flipping. Remember, a property's outdoor space is an extension of its living area, and enhancing it can significantly impact the property's appeal and value.

Keep an Eye on Resale Value: Always Consider the End Goal

Prioritizing Resale Value in House Flipping: In house flipping, the primary objective is to sell the property at a profit. Therefore, keeping a constant eye on the potential resale value is crucial. This section emphasizes the importance of considering the end goal – resale value – in every decision made during the house flipping process.

Why Resale Value is Key:

Guides Renovation Decisions: Understanding what adds value helps in making smart renovation choices, ensuring that investments contribute to an increased resale price.

Determines Project Scope: Focusing on resale value helps in defining the scope of the project, preventing over-improvement or under-improvement of the property.

Influences Budget Allocation: Resale value considerations guide how and where to allocate the budget to get the best return on investment.

Strategies to Maximize Resale Value:

Market Research: Conduct thorough market research to understand what features and improvements are most valued in the local real estate market.

Target Buyer Demographics: Tailor the property to appeal to the most likely buyer demographic in the area, whether it's families, young professionals, or retirees.

Cost-Effective Renovations: Focus on renovations that offer the highest return on investment. Often, simple cosmetic updates can significantly boost resale value.

Quality Workmanship: Ensure that all renovations are done with quality workmanship. Shoddy work can decrease the property's value and lead to longer sale times.

Curb Appeal: Invest in the property's exterior and landscaping, as curb appeal significantly impacts a buyer's first impression.

Neutral and Appealing Design Choices: Opt for neutral and broadly appealing design choices that can attract a wide range of buyers.

Stay Within Budget: Keep a close eye on the budget to avoid overspending, as this can cut into your profit margins.

The Role of Resale Value in Decision-Making: Every decision, from paint colors to fixture selections, should be made with an eye on how it will affect the property's resale value. It's a balance of appeal, cost, and market trends.

Conclusion:

 In house flipping, the resale value should be the guiding force behind every decision. By consistently focusing on the end goal, you can make strategic choices that enhance the property's appeal and marketability, ensuring a profitable and successful flip. Remember, in real estate investing, the ultimate measure of success is the return on investment at resale, making it imperative to keep resale value at the forefront of your flipping strategy.

Learn from Mistakes: Use Each Project as a Learning Experience

The Role of Mistakes in House Flipping: Mistakes are an inevitable part of the house flipping process, especially for those new to the field. Rather than being discouraged by these setbacks, successful house flippers use them as valuable learning experiences. This section emphasizes the importance of learning from mistakes and how this approach can enhance your skills and strategies in future projects.

Why Learning from Mistakes is Important:

Improves Decision-Making: Analyzing past mistakes helps in making more informed decisions in future projects, reducing the likelihood of repeating the same errors.

Enhances Skills and Knowledge: Each mistake is an opportunity to deepen your understanding of house flipping, from renovation techniques to market trends.

Builds Resilience: Learning from mistakes fosters resilience, an essential trait for navigating the ups and downs of real estate investing.

Strategies for Learning from Mistakes:

Reflect and Analyze: After each project, take time to reflect on what went well and what didn't. Identify the mistakes and analyze the reasons behind them.

Document Lessons Learned: Keep a record of the lessons learned from each project. This can serve as a reference for future projects and help avoid repeating mistakes.

Seek Feedback: Don't hesitate to ask for feedback from your team, contractors, or real estate agents. They can offer different perspectives on what could have been done better.

Stay Open to Learning: Maintain an open and growth-oriented mindset. Be willing to learn from others, including fellow flippers, mentors, and industry experts.

Implement Changes: Use the insights gained from past mistakes to improve your processes, from planning and budgeting to execution and sales.

Share Your Experiences: Sharing your experiences, both successes and failures, with others can be educational for both you and your peers.

The Impact of Embracing Mistakes: Embracing and learning from mistakes can significantly improve your efficiency, effectiveness, and success rate in house flipping. It leads to continuous improvement and helps build a more robust and knowledgeable approach to real estate investing.

Conclusion:

Mistakes in house flipping are not just setbacks; they are stepping stones to success. By learning from each experience, you can continually refine your strategies, improve your skills, and increase your chances of success in future projects. Remember, the most successful house flippers are those who view every project as an opportunity to learn, grow, and develop their expertise.

Stay Legally Compliant: Ensure All Work Meets Legal Standards

The Necessity of Legal Compliance in House Flipping:
Legal compliance is a crucial aspect of house flipping. Ensuring that all renovation work meets legal and regulatory standards not only protects you from potential liabilities but also assures the safety and satisfaction of future homeowners. This section highlights the importance of adhering to legal requirements in house flipping and how to effectively manage this aspect.

Why Legal Compliance is Critical:

Avoiding Legal Issues: Non-compliance with building codes, zoning laws, and permit requirements can lead to legal complications, including fines and project delays.

Ensuring Safety: Compliance with legal standards ensures that renovation work is safe for occupants and meets health and safety regulations.

Market Reputation: Legally compliant renovations enhance your reputation as a responsible and trustworthy house flipper.

Strategies for Ensuring Legal Compliance:

Understand Local Building Codes: Familiarize yourself with the local building codes and regulations. These can vary significantly from one region to another.

Obtain Necessary Permits: Ensure that all necessary permits are obtained before starting any renovation work. This includes permits for structural changes, electrical work, plumbing, and more.

Work with Licensed Professionals: Hire licensed contractors and tradespeople who are familiar with the local building codes and legal requirements.

Regular Inspections: Have the renovation work inspected regularly by certified inspectors to ensure compliance.

Stay Informed: Keep up-to-date with changes in building codes and regulations. Attending local real estate and construction seminars can be beneficial.

Document Compliance: Keep detailed records of permits, inspections, and work done. This documentation can be valuable in case of future legal inquiries.

The Role of Legal Compliance in Project Success: Staying legally compliant helps ensure the smooth progression of your flipping project. It also builds confidence among potential buyers regarding the quality and legality of the renovation work.

Conclusion:

In house flipping, legal compliance is not just a legal obligation but a key component of project success. It ensures the integrity and safety of your renovation projects and protects your investment. By prioritizing legal compliance, you can avoid potential legal pitfalls and establish your credibility as a professional house flipper. Remember, in real estate, a strong commitment to legal compliance is an integral part of building a sustainable and reputable business.

Prioritize Safety: Ensure Safe Practices During Renovations

The Importance of Safety in House Flipping: Safety is paramount in the house flipping process. Prioritizing safe practices during renovations not only protects those working on the project but also ensures the long-term safety of future homeowners. This section discusses the significance of safety measures and how to effectively implement them in your renovation projects.

Why Safety is a Priority:

Protection of Workers: Ensuring the safety of contractors and workers helps prevent accidents and injuries, promoting a healthy work environment.

Quality Workmanship: Safe renovation practices often lead to better quality work, as they encourage attention to detail and careful execution.

Legal Compliance: Adhering to safety regulations is a legal requirement. Non-compliance can lead to fines, legal issues, and project delays.

Reputation: A commitment to safety enhances your reputation as a responsible and professional house flipper.

Implementing Safety Practices:

Use of Personal Protective Equipment (PPE): Ensure that everyone on site uses appropriate safety gear, such as helmets, goggles, gloves, and safety boots.

Proper Training: Provide training for workers on safe practices, proper use of tools and equipment, and awareness of potential hazards.

Regular Safety Inspections: Conduct regular inspections of the work site to identify and address potential safety hazards.

Organized Worksite: Keep the renovation area tidy and organized to reduce the risk of accidents, such as trips and falls.

Emergency Preparedness: Have a plan in place for emergencies, including first-aid kits, fire extinguishers, and clear evacuation routes.

Safe Handling of Materials: Ensure safe storage and handling of construction materials, especially hazardous substances like paint and solvents.

Compliance with Regulations: Stay informed about and comply with all relevant safety regulations and building codes.

The Role of Safety in Project Success: Prioritizing safety contributes to the smooth and efficient completion of renovation projects. It creates a positive and secure work environment, which can lead to better productivity and higher-quality outcomes.

Conclusion:

In house flipping, safety should never be an afterthought. Prioritizing safe practices is essential for the wellbeing of workers and the success of your projects. By implementing rigorous safety measures, you not only protect your team but also demonstrate a commitment to professionalism and quality. Remember, in the business of house flipping, a safe project is a successful project.

Keep Up with Industry News: Stay Updated on Real Estate and Construction News

In the ever-evolving world of house flipping, staying abreast of the latest real estate and construction news is not just beneficial—it's essential. Here's how you can keep your finger on the pulse of the industry:

1. Subscribe to Industry Publications and Websites

Real Estate Journals: Look for publications that focus on market trends, property values, and regional growth.

Construction Updates: Stay informed about new construction methods, materials, and regulations.

Online Forums and Blogs: Join online communities where professionals discuss the latest news and share insights.

2. Follow Market Statistics and Reports

Housing Market Reports: Regularly check for updates on housing prices, supply and demand dynamics, and consumer preferences.

Economic Indicators: Understand how broader economic trends impact the real estate market.

3. Attend Industry Events and Webinars

Conferences and Seminars: These are great places to network and learn from experts.

Webinars and Online Courses: These can provide in-depth knowledge without the need to travel.

4. Network with Industry Professionals

Local Real Estate Groups: Join these groups to share experiences and get localized advice.

Social Media Groups: Platforms like LinkedIn and Facebook have numerous groups dedicated to real estate and construction.

5. Utilize Technology and Tools

Apps and Software: There are many applications designed to provide real-time updates on market trends and construction advancements.

6. Set Up News Alerts

Custom Alerts: Use services like Google Alerts to get notified about specific topics of interest in real estate and construction.

7. Read Case Studies and Success Stories

Learning from Others: Understand how successful flippers navigate the market and adapt to changes.

8. Regular Review and Analysis

Reflect on Information: Regularly review the information you gather and analyze how it applies to your current and future projects.

Actionable Steps:

Create a Reading Schedule: Dedicate a specific time each day or week to catch up on industry news.

Summarize Key Takeaways: After each reading session, jot down key points that could impact your flipping strategies.

Stay Curious: Always be on the lookout for new sources of information and perspectives.

Summary:

Keeping up with industry news in real estate and construction equips you with the knowledge to make informed decisions, foresee market trends, and stay ahead of the competition. By dedicating time to understand the market dynamics, you position yourself for greater success in your house flipping endeavors.

Next Steps:

- Start by subscribing to a couple of industry-leading publications today.
- Join a webinar this month to deepen your understanding of a specific aspect of house flipping.
- Set up news alerts on key topics relevant to your market.

Remember, knowledge is power in the fast-paced world of house flipping! Stay informed, stay ahead.

Choose the Right Sales Strategy: Determine the best way to market and sell

Selecting an effective sales strategy is crucial for the success of your house flipping project. Here's how to approach it:

Understanding Your Market: Start by getting to know your target buyers and local market trends. Are you selling to families, young professionals, or retirees? What features and styles are currently in demand in your area? This knowledge will guide your entire sales approach.

Preparing the Property: Make your house appealing to potential buyers. This involves staging it attractively, which may require a professional's touch. Also, invest in high-quality photography for your listings; good visuals make a significant difference.

Listing the Property: You have several options here. Online listings can reach a broad audience quickly. Working with a real estate agent can provide valuable market insights and negotiation skills. Alternatively, a For Sale By Owner (FSBO) approach can save on fees but demands more effort and understanding of the selling process.

Effective Marketing: Utilize various channels for marketing. Social media platforms can be powerful tools for reaching potential buyers. Hosting open houses allows people to experience the property firsthand. Don't underestimate the power of word-of-mouth; let your personal and professional networks know about your listing.

Pricing Strategy: Setting the right price is a delicate balance. Research comparable properties in your area to set a competitive price. Be open to adjusting your price based on how the market responds to your listing.

Negotiation Skills: Be clear on your bottom line but remain open to negotiation. Responding promptly to offers and showing a willingness to engage can help close the deal faster.

Closing the Deal: Ensure all legal and financial aspects of the sale are handled correctly. Working with a trusted closing agent can facilitate a smooth transaction.

Summary

Your sales strategy should be a well-thought-out plan that considers market dynamics, effective property presentation, strategic pricing, and skilled negotiation. By meticulously preparing and executing each step of this plan, you increase your chances of a profitable and timely sale.

Next Steps

- Conduct thorough market research to understand your target demographic and local trends.
- Allocate resources for property staging and professional photography.
- Develop a comprehensive marketing plan, including listing details and promotional activities.

- The right sales strategy transforms your house flipping project from mere potential to a profitable reality. Remember, a well-marketed and strategically sold property is the cornerstone of successful house flipping.

Utilize Social Media: Leveraging Online Platforms for Marketing

In the digital age, social media is a powerful tool for marketing your house flipping projects. Here's how to effectively use these platforms:

Develop a Strong Online Presence: Create dedicated profiles for your house flipping business on popular social media platforms like Facebook, Instagram, and Twitter. These profiles should reflect your brand and showcase your projects.

Showcase Your Projects: Use social media to post before-and-after photos, progress updates, and behind-the-scenes glimpses into your flipping process. This not only builds interest but also establishes your credibility in the field.

Engage with Your Audience: Social media is not just about broadcasting; it's about engaging. Respond to comments, participate in relevant conversations, and even ask for feedback. This interaction builds community and trust among your followers.

Utilize Paid Advertising: Platforms like Facebook and Instagram offer targeted advertising options. These can be highly effective in reaching potential buyers in your area or those interested in real estate investments.

Leverage Video Content: Platforms like YouTube or Instagram Reels are excellent for sharing more in-depth content. Consider creating virtual tours of your properties or educational content about house flipping.

Collaborate with Influencers: Partnering with local influencers or real estate personalities can amplify your reach. Choose collaborators who align with your brand and have an audience that would be interested in your projects.

Track and Analyze Performance: Use the analytics tools provided by social media platforms to track the performance of your posts. Understanding what type of content resonates with your audience can help you refine your strategy.

Summary

Social media is an invaluable asset in your house flipping toolkit. It allows you to reach a broad audience, showcase your work, and build a community around your brand. By strategically using these platforms, you can significantly enhance the visibility and appeal of your properties.

Next Steps

- Set up business profiles on key social media platforms.
- Plan a content calendar with regular updates and varied content types.
- Explore paid advertising options for targeted reach.

In the dynamic world of house flipping, social media is not just a trend but a vital component of a successful marketing strategy. Engaging effectively on these platforms can transform the way you connect with potential buyers and the wider real estate community.

Practice Ethical Investing: Maintaining Integrity in Your Business Dealings

Ethical investing in house flipping is not just about making profits; it's about doing so responsibly and with integrity. Here's how to ensure your business practices reflect these values:

Transparency with Buyers and Sellers: Be honest and upfront in all your transactions. This includes providing complete and accurate information about properties, disclosing any potential issues, and being clear about pricing and terms.

Fair Treatment of Contractors and Employees: Ensure that everyone involved in your flipping projects, from contractors to support staff, is treated fairly and respectfully. This includes providing fair wages, safe working conditions, and clear communication.

Responsible Renovations: When renovating properties, consider the impact on the environment and the community. Use sustainable materials when possible and respect the architectural integrity and history of the neighborhood.

Community Engagement: Be mindful of how your investments affect the local community. Engaging with community members and participating in local events can foster goodwill and a positive reputation.

Upholding Legal and Ethical Standards: Stay informed about the laws and regulations governing real estate and construction in your area. Adhere strictly to these rules to avoid legal issues and maintain a reputation for integrity.

Dealing with Conflict: If conflicts arise, address them fairly and ethically. This might involve mediation or other conflict resolution strategies to ensure all parties are heard and respected.

Summary

Ethical investing in house flipping is about balancing profit with integrity, transparency, and responsibility. By adhering to these principles, you not only enhance your reputation but also contribute positively to the communities in which you work.

Next Steps

- Review your current business practices for any ethical gaps.
- Engage with local communities to understand their needs and perspectives.
- Attend a workshop or seminar on ethical business practices in real estate.

Incorporating ethical practices into your house flipping business is not just good for your conscience; it's good for your brand and can lead to long-term success and respect in the industry.

Build Good Relationships with Suppliers: Securing Good Terms and Prices

Building strong relationships with suppliers is key to securing favorable terms and prices for your house flipping projects. Here's how to cultivate these valuable connections:

Understand Their Business: Learn about your suppliers' operations, challenges, and goals. This understanding can help you align your requests with their capabilities and constraints, leading to better negotiations.

Regular Communication: Maintain open and consistent communication. Regular check-ins, feedback, and discussions about future needs and projects can foster a sense of partnership.

Timely Payments: Pay your bills on time. Reliable payment is one of the most effective ways to build trust and goodwill with suppliers.

Bulk Purchases and Long-Term Contracts: If possible, consolidate your purchases. Larger orders or long-term commitments can often secure better pricing or terms.

Mutual Respect and Professionalism: Treat your suppliers as valued partners. Respectful and professional interactions set the tone for a positive long-term relationship.

Flexibility and Understanding: Be flexible and understanding in your dealings. If a supplier faces a challenge or delay, working together to find a solution can strengthen the relationship.

Referrals and Recommendations: If you're pleased with a supplier's work, refer them to others. Positive word-of-mouth can be beneficial for their business and can also make them more inclined to offer you favorable terms.

Summary

Good supplier relationships are about more than just getting the lowest price; they're about creating mutually beneficial partnerships. These connections can lead to better service, quality, and terms, which can significantly impact the success and profitability of your house flipping endeavors.

Next Steps

- Schedule meetings with your current suppliers to discuss future projects and needs.
- Explore opportunities for bulk purchases or long-term contracts.
- Set up a system to ensure timely payments to your suppliers.

Remember, in the house flipping business, your network of suppliers is a critical asset. Investing time and effort in these relationships can yield substantial returns in the form of reliable supply chains, quality materials, and favorable pricing.

Know Your Limits: Don't Take on More Than You Can Handle

In the world of house flipping, it's crucial to recognize and respect your limits. Overextending can lead to financial strain, decreased quality of work, and increased stress. Here's how to manage your projects wisely:

Realistic Project Assessment: Before taking on a new project, assess it realistically in terms of your available time, finances, and skills. Consider the scale of the renovation, the condition of the property, and your current workload.

Financial Prudence: Be cautious with your finances. Avoid over-leveraging yourself with too many loans or credit lines. Maintain a budget for each project and include a contingency fund for unexpected expenses.

Time Management: Understand the time commitment each project requires. Consider not just the renovation work but also the time needed for planning, sourcing materials, and marketing the property.

Skill Evaluation: Be honest about your skills and expertise. If a project requires skills beyond your current capabilities, consider bringing in experts or taking the time to learn before diving in.

Stress and Health Considerations: Pay attention to your stress levels and overall health. House flipping can be demanding, so it's important to know when to take a step back and prioritize your well-being.

Seeking Advice and Support: Don't hesitate to seek advice from more experienced flippers or mentors. A second opinion can help you gauge whether a project is manageable.

Summary

Knowing your limits is about balancing ambition with a realistic understanding of your resources and capabilities. By carefully evaluating each potential project and recognizing your own boundaries, you can avoid overextension and ensure the sustainability of your house flipping business.

Next Steps

- Review your current and planned projects to evaluate if they align with your capacity.
- Create a checklist for assessing future projects, including financial, time, and skill considerations.
- Schedule regular check-ins with yourself to monitor your stress levels and overall workload.

In house flipping, success is not just about the quantity of projects completed but the quality and profitability of each one. Understanding and respecting your limits is key to maintaining a successful and enjoyable career in this field.

Regularly Review Finances: Keeping Track of Expenses and Profits

In house flipping, financial management is as crucial as the actual renovation work. Regularly reviewing your finances ensures that you stay on budget and can help maximize profits. Here's how to effectively manage your financial tracking:

Set Up a Tracking System: Use accounting software or a spreadsheet to track all your expenses and income. This system should be easy to update and review.

Categorize Your Expenses: Break down your expenses into categories such as materials, labor, marketing, and unexpected costs. This categorization helps in identifying areas where you might be overspending.

Monitor Cash Flow: Keep an eye on the cash flow of your projects. This includes tracking when expenses are due and when you can expect returns from sales.

Regular Reviews: Schedule regular times to review your finances. This could be weekly, bi-weekly, or monthly, depending on the scale of your operations.

Budget for Each Project: Create a detailed budget for each flipping project and stick to it as closely as possible. Include a contingency fund for unexpected expenses.

Analyze Profit and Loss: After selling a property, conduct a profit and loss analysis. This helps you understand what worked well and where you can improve in future projects.

Seek Professional Advice: Don't hesitate to consult with a financial advisor, especially when dealing with complex financial decisions or tax implications.

Summary

Regular financial reviews are essential for maintaining control over your house flipping projects and ensuring their profitability. By keeping a close eye on expenses, cash flow, and overall budgeting, you can make informed decisions that will positively impact your bottom line.

Next Steps

- Implement a financial tracking system if you haven't already.
- Schedule your next financial review session and make it a regular part of your routine.
- After your next sale, take the time to thoroughly analyze the financial outcome of the project.

Remember, effective financial management is a key factor in the success of your house flipping endeavors. Staying organized and informed about your financial status enables you to make smarter investment choices and ultimately leads to greater profitability.

Be Mindful of Trends: Understanding Current Design and Amenity Trends

Staying informed about current design and amenity trends is crucial in house flipping. It ensures your properties meet buyer expectations and stand out in the market. Here's how to keep up with the latest trends:

Research Online and Print Media: Regularly browse interior design websites, follow relevant social media accounts, and subscribe to home renovation magazines. These resources are rich in current trends and design inspiration.

Attend Trade Shows and Expos: Trade shows and expos are great for seeing the latest designs and amenities firsthand. They provide insights into emerging trends and popular materials.

Network with Industry Professionals: Connect with interior designers, architects, and contractors who can provide valuable insights into what's trending in home design.

Understand Your Market: Trends can vary significantly depending on the region and target demographic. Conduct market research to understand what appeals to buyers in your area.

Incorporate Sustainable and Tech-Friendly Features: Sustainability and technology are increasingly important to modern homebuyers. Consider eco-friendly materials and smart home features in your renovations.

Balance Trends with Timelessness: While it's important to be trendy, ensure that your designs also have a timeless appeal. Avoid overly bold choices that might not age well.

Visit Show Homes and Local Listings: Explore show homes and local listings to see how other properties are being designed and marketed.

Summary

Being mindful of current trends in design and amenities allows you to create properties that resonate with today's buyers. By blending modern trends with timeless elements, you can enhance the appeal and marketability of your flipped homes.

Next Steps

- Schedule regular sessions for online research and reading on the latest home design trends.
- Plan to attend upcoming trade shows or design expos.
- Arrange meetings with design professionals to discuss current and upcoming trends.

In the dynamic world of house flipping, an understanding of current trends is a valuable tool. It enables you to create spaces that not only look great but also meet the evolving preferences and needs of homebuyers.

Conclusion

As we close the final pages of this journey into the world of house flipping, it's important to reflect on the key insights and strategies we've explored. From understanding the nuances of the real estate market to discussing the art of renovation and sale, this book has aimed to equip you with the essential knowledge and tools for your house flipping endeavors.

Remember, success in house flipping is not just about making profitable investments; it's also about learning from experiences, adapting to changing markets, and making informed decisions. The stories, tips, and checklists provided here are meant to guide you, but your journey will be unique, filled with its own challenges and triumphs.

As you step out and apply these lessons, keep in mind that patience, diligence, and continuous learning are your best allies. Stay updated with market trends, be meticulous in your planning, and always be prepared to adapt your strategies.

Here's to turning houses into homes and investments into successes!

ABOUT THE AUTHOR

Anthony Dallas is a hobby researcher, writer, and developer with an interest in how technology shapes our world and the use of technology to enhance communication and creativity.